GOV. JERRY BROWN'S DESTRUCTION OF THE CALIFORNIA JUDICIARY

Originally written by

Louis Wm. Barnett

John M. Feliz

Dave Scholl

Renewed by Louis Wm. Barnett

1

Photo cover by
    Jupiter Images

Copies of this book may be purchased for $9.95. All inquiries
should be emailed to LouisWBarnett@yahoo.com.

DEDICATION

To the hundreds of fine men and women, of varying talent, education and experience, who individually pursue the just application of the law as it is written – rather than as they may personally feel it should have been written.

TABLE OF CONTENTS

FORWARD

Government has no greater responsibility to its citizens than the protection of their life, liberty and property.

That is the principal reason that Jerry Brown's governorship was such a tragedy.

Few people today remember his personal friend, campaign chauffeur, cabinet member, and Chief Justice of the California State Supreme Court Rose Elizabeth Bird. Her ten years as Chief Justice, with no prior judicial experience, marked a decline in public safety for all Californians.

Over ten years as California's 25th Chief Justice, Rose Bird reviewed 56 capital cases appealed to the California State Supreme Court. She categorically opposed the death penalty and voted to overturn every single death penalty decision. Critics of Bird charged that her personal opposition to the death penalty was more important to her (and to Brown who appointed her and who also opposed the death penalty) than the laws and precedents upon which judicial decisions are based. The Bird court also ruled unconstitutional California's "use a gun, go to jail" law which made a prison term mandatory for any crime in which a gun was used.

Chief Justice Rose Bird became a symbol of liberal justice.

Twelve years after her defeat in November of 1986, a fellow Supreme Court Justice, Stanley Mosk gave an inside perspective on Justice Bird:

"Rose Bird was pilloried because she generally voted to find some defect in death penalty convictions and to reverse them. I probably don't like the death penalty any more than she does. As a matter of fact, I think the death penalty is wrong ...... But the difference is that I took an oath to support the law as it is and not as I might prefer it to be, and therefore, I've written my share of opinions upholding capital judgments."

Capital cases were not Rose Bird's only liberal decisions. She issued political and unconstitutional rulings. In one case, liberal Democrats in the state legislature passed a redistricting plan to draw safe districts for themselves and deny the voters any opportunity to defeat them. The California Constitution allows the people to circulate petitions (which they did) and prevent a bill from becoming law. Bird violated the Constitution by ordering those lines to be used in the 1982 election.

But it wasn't just California's crime victims and private citizens whose rights were violated.

The California State Constitution requires judges to issue decisions within 90 days. Making a mockery of the law, Rose Bird held that the 90 days did not begin until they were ready to file their decision.

Gov. Jerry Brown's State Controller could have withheld the Court's pay until they complied with the Constitution but, instead, the Governor's liberal cohort not only continued to pay the judges , but also defended his decision in court. The legacy of Jerry Brown's judicial appointments to this day remains a challenge to the defense of life, liberty and property for Californians.

— Senator Tony Strickland

ACKNOWLEDGEMENTS

The authors wish to express their gratitude to the people who made this book possible. In particular, we thank the attorneys, police officers, judges (sitting and retired), and deputy district attorneys (especially those in Alameda, Fresno, Los Angeles, Orange, Sacramento, San Diego, and Santa Clara counties). We also thank the reporters and library staff of the *San Fernando Daily News*, the *San Jose Mercury News*, the *Oakland Tribune*, the *Pasadena Star-News*, the *Orange County Register*, and the *Santa Rosa Press Democrat*. Thanks also to those organizations concerned with the quality of the judicial system — Citizens for Law and Order, the United States Justice Foundation, the Law and Order Campaign Committee, and the Republican Associates of Los Angeles.

Numerous individuals were most helpful in aiding us in preparing this book, including Jan Drenth, Matt Potthast, Homer Young, Carl Olson, the very professional career staffs of the various courts, the Administrative Judicial Council — as well as numerous current and former colleagues of the California Chief Justice.

We thank Justice L. Thaxton Hanson of the Court of Appeals; The Honorable Edwin Meese, III; the family of William E. James; and Judge Clyde Small for their permission to edit and include their articles in this book.

A special debt of gratitude is owed to Bob Levy who edited most of these articles.

The personal interest and professional guidance of Jameson G. Campaigne, Jr. was instrumental in the original publication of this book.

Any contribution which this book makes to the public dialogue on the California judicial system is due to the many, many people who provided guidance, information, help and moral support.

Any shortcomings which this book exhibits are the responsibility of the authors themselves who gathered the stories, pieced together the information, verified the facts, and crafted the words.

PROLOGUE

The California court system was once regarded by legal scholars as the premier court system in the United States.

How the California Supreme Court and the state's lower courts fell from this high status is a matter of dispute.

Some — mostly prosecutors and police — find the cause of the fall to be judicial leniency and activism.

Others — mostly judges and defense attorneys — find fault with the press and judicial critics, especially those in elected office. They blame the press for unflattering articles about the bench and charge that the critics are attempting to infringe on the independence of the judiciary.

The purpose of this book is to set forth clear and simple facts which speak for themselves.

The first fact is that the decline of the reputation of the California judiciary clearly coincides with the election of Jerry Brown as Governor of the state.

The results of which are Jerry Brown's judicial legacy.

Rodney Alcala – Serial Killer

Rodney James Alcala, was convicted in Orange County on March 9, 2010 of five murders and rapes. Alcala is the serial killer dubbed "The Dating Game Killer" for his appearance on the television show The Dating Game in the 1970s. The winner on the show became the real winner when she declined the date with Alcala.

A graduate of UCLA's School of Fine Arts with an IQ equivalent to Albert Einstein, Alcala also attended New York University under an alias (John Berger), and studied film under Roman Polanski.

Shockingly, the March 9, 2010 conviction is Alcala's third death sentence for the same crime, the murder of 12-year-old Robin Samsoe.

But the story begins earlier, in 1968, when Alcala raped an eight-year-old in his apartment and bashed her in the head with a pipe. The young girl, identified only as Tali S, was saved due to the actions of a private citizen – a Good

Samaritan - who saw Alcala luring a child, followed them, and called the police. Tali S was found raped and battered on the floor in Alcala's apartment. He fled when the police arrived.

Alcala hid in New Hampshire working as a counselor at an arts camp for teenagers. He was identified as one of the FBI's 10 Most Wanted and arrested on August 12, 1971. Returned to California, Alcala was convicted in 1972 under California's indeterminate sentencing law which was supposed to rehabilitate criminals. Despite the rape and battery with a pipe of an eight-year-old, Alcala was released in 1974 after only 34 months in prison.

Less than two months after his release, authorities found Alcala with a 13-year-old girl who said Alcala had kidnapped her. Alcala was convicted of violating his parole and providing marijuana to a minor, and incarcerated for two years.

After his release and despite being a registered sex-offender, his Parole Officer allowed Alcala to travel to New York. He is currently the prime suspect in the murder of a young socialite, piano virtuoso Ellen Jane Hoover, who had written "John Berger" on her calendar for the day she disappeared. John Berger was Alcala's alias when he was attending New York University and hiding in New Hampshire. A ponytailed photographer (a match for Alcala) named John Berger was the last person seen with her. The murder occurred approximately a week after his arrival in New York. Alcala is also a suspect in the 1971 murder of a TWA flight attendant in New York at a time when Alcala was living in New Hampshire.

Robin Samsoe, a 12-year-old Huntington Beach girl with blond hair and blue eyes was Alcala's first murder indictment. On June 20, 1979, Robin and her friend, Bridgette, had been approached by Alcala who tried to take their pictures. Robin and her friend knew better and left for her friend's house. Once there, Robin borrowed her friend's bike and left for her ballet class. 12 days later, Robin's body was found in the Los Angeles Foothills.

Her young body was discovered by rangers who mistook her body for that of an animal because her arms and legs were gone. They played catch with the bones until they realized that the skull did not belong to an animal but belonged to a child.

When Alcala was arrested, officers discovered that he

had a locker in Seattle, Washington, which contained thousands of pictures of young girls and Robin's earring along with many other pairs of earrings according to Robin's mother, Marianne Frazier.

Alcala was convicted and, on June 20th, 1980, Alcala was sentenced to death for the rape and murder of 12-year-old Robin Samsoe. The judge, in pronouncing the verdict, said Alcala was "vicious, evil (and) malevolent." In September of that year, Alcala also was convicted in the 1978 rape of a 15-year-old Riverside girl and received a nine year sentence.

The Samsoe conviction which, under Rose Bird, on August 23, 1984, overturned Alcala's conviction. The decision was written by fellow Jerry Brown appointee, Justice Joseph R. Grodin. Justice Stanley Mosk, a Democrat and former California State Attorney General, dissented.

Two years later, in 1986, Alcala was again, for the second time, convicted of Samsoe's rape and murder in a trial that put Robin Samsoe's family through an ordeal that Robin's mother found worse than the first trial.

In 2001, Alcala's appeals reached the United States Ninth Circuit Court of Appeals. The Ninth Circuit has the most liberal judges of any Circuit in the United States – judges akin to Rose Bird - and is the Circuit most reversed by the United States Supreme Court. Sadly, Alcala's appeal paid off and his conviction was again overturned 22 years after he murdered Robin Samsoe.

In 2003, as the Orange County District Attorney's office worked on a new strategy for Alcala's third prosecution and trial, Los Angeles County District Attorney Steve Cooley's office contacted Orange County Senior Deputy District Attorney Murphy and changed the course of Alcala's third trial. Cooley's office had found that the DNA taken from Alcala's mouth – over his objections – matched the DNA in semen left on two rape-murder victims in the West LA area. His DNA matched that found on Georgia Wixted, a 27 year old nurse found in Malibu on December 16, 1977, and semen left on Charlotte Lamb, 32, a Santa Monica legal secretary found in her El Segundo laundry room on June 24, 1978. Both women's bodies were in "eerie, artfully posed positions" according to the LA Weekly, January 21, 2010. Alcala, a photographer, had photographed many women who authorities are still trying to identify.

In 2004, Alcala's DNA was traced to semen on the carefully posed body of Jill Barcomb, an 18-year-old runaway who Alcala picked up on Sunset Boulevard. Jill Barcomb was found on November 10, 1977 on a dirt road near Mulholland Drive not far from Marlon Brando's home. Investigators believe Alcala may be guilty of additional murders and possibly as many as 30 including the two in New York. When investigations are completed, Alcala may be found to be the worst serial killer in American history.

At one point, Alcala had pled guilty by reason of insanity in the murders of Georgia Wixted, Charlotte Lamb, Jill Barcomb, and Jill Parenteau who was found murdered in her Burbank apartment just six days before Robin Samsoe's abduction.

While insane by any common definition of human decency, Alcala was not only a serial rapist and murderer, he would strangle his victims, then revive them so that he could strangle them again. As criminals go, he was a true monster.

Alcala sued the State of California prison system for not feeding him low fat food and again for a slip-and-fall claim.

He also challenged the taking of his DNA in prison without his permission as an infringement on his rights. It is undoubtedly a good thing that Chief Justice Rose Bird became the first state Supreme Court justice in American history to be defeated in a retention election in 1986 by an overwhelming margin of 67% to 33% before this argument could be brought before the Bird Court. Remember, Chief Justice Bird in all 56 death penalty cases brought before her court voted to overturn the death penalty in every single case.

Robert Samsoe, Robin's brother who was 13 when Robin was killed, was quoted in the LA Weekly article as saying "I don't have any faith in the system. Some people ... are just offered all the chances in the world, Alcala cost ... California more than any other person because of his lawsuits. And they treat him like a king. Everyone is walking on pins and needles around him."

25 years – almost a generation - after the defeat of Chief Justice Rose Bird and her liberal colleagues in the November 4, 1984 general election, justice may finally have been served in the case of Rodney Alcala. However, the decisions that Chief Justice Rose Bird's Court set in the Alcala case and other cases remain the law of the State of California.

PART I

LOWERING THE LOWER COURTS

CHAPTER ONE

THE HIGH COURT

When the police went to investigate a burglary in fashionable Oakland Hills, they didn't realize the controversy that was about to begin. Mrs. Deborah Halvonik, who had reported the burglary, invited the officers into her home and told them about the television and video tape recorder that had been stolen. But while they were looking for clues to the crime, the officers saw two growing marijuana plants.

The next day, September 18, 1979, Oakland Narcotics Sgt. Larry Rodrigue found a memo from the officers on his desk about the plants.

On Wednesday, the 19th, Rodrigue and Officer James Kinsey drove to the Halvoniks' neighborhood. Using a 15 power telescope, Rodrigue saw a wooden planter on the upper level deck which appeared to have marijuana plants growing in it.

Rodrigue and Kinsey went to Municipal Judge Robert Friborg and obtained a warrant to search the Halvonik home. At 3:30 that afternoon, Rodrigue called the Halvoniks to be sure they would be there. He told them that he would be over to discuss the burglary.

At 7:30 that evening, Rodrigue led a team of seven other officers on a raid of the Halvonik residence. Sgt. Rodrigue promised the Halvoniks that they would search the home "as neatly as possible."[1]

The search turned up 323 live marijuana plants, a couple bags of smokable marijuana, and one-third of an ounce of cocaine. [2]

The Halvoniks were charged with possession of cocaine, cultivating marijuana, and possessing marijuana for sale. But instead of being brought to the police station for normal booking procedures, the Halvoniks were released on their own recognizance, pending formal charging and arraignment.[3]

The Halvoniks, it turned out, were not just ordinary sophisticated upper-middle class drug abusers. Paul N. Halvonik was a Justice of the California State Court of Appeals in San Francisco — the second highest court in the state's judicial system. He was also known to be a leading contender for the next vacancy on the California State Supreme Court.

Judge Halvonik, a long time friend and political ally of Jerry Brown, had been appointed by the governor to the Appeal Court bench in 1978. He was confirmed, in a swirl of controversy, by a two to one vote of the California Commission on Judicial Appointments on May 26, 1978. During the Commission's review, it was learned that Paul Halvonik had an earlier brush with drug laws at San Quentin on July 10, 1974. Halvonik, then a lawyer representing an inmate at the prison, was caught with a home-rolled marijuana cigarette in his possession.[4]

It is a felony to attempt to bring contraband into a prison. At that time possession of marijuana was also a felony. The officer who discovered the marijuana joint described Halvonik as "glassy-eyed." When Halvonik was asked about the joint, he denied knowing anything about it — even though it was inside his own pack of Marlboros.[5] The matter was turned over to Marin County Deputy District Attorney, Ernest Zunino, Chief of the Investigative Complaints Division. Zunino decided not to prosecute because of a lack of sufficient evidence to prove "knowing possession." But he warned Paul Halvonik not to let it happen again. Halvonik promised it wouldn't.

As an attorney, of course, Halvonik couldn't claim ignorance of the law. In fact, he had been deeply involved in legal actions regarding drugs. In 1970, he brought suit to reinstate the teaching credential of a man who had been arrested for possession of marijuana. In 1973, Halvonik was hired by the City of Berkeley to defend an initiative liberalizing the city's marijuana laws. The state at the time was challenging the legality of such a liberalization.

Despite Halvonik's background, the Commission on Judicial Appointments approved him for the Court of Appeal. Voting to confirm him was Chief Justice of the California State Supreme Court, Rose Bird — another Jerry Brown appointee. Joining her was Wakefield Taylor, senior presiding judge of the First District Court of Appeal. The one vote against Halvonik was cast by then Attorney General Evelle

Younger, who was convinced that Paul Halvonik had knowingly possessed the marijuana joint in question.[6]

Just a year and four months after his appointment, Halvonik was charged with the Oakland offenses. Embarrassed by his appointee, Jerry Brown tried to cut his own losses. During a television interview on KNBC in Los Angeles, Brown claimed Halvonik was just one of hundreds of appointments he had to make as governor. It wouldn't be fair, he argued, for another to blame him if one or two appointees ran afoul of the law.[7]

What a cruel way to disown an old friend! For Paul Halvonik was not just some obscure appointee. He and Jerry Brown had been intimate associates since 1964, when they had been in the same car pool commuting from Berkeley to San Francisco.

Also in the car pool was J. Anthony Kline. Kline was Halvonik's roommate in Berkeley, and had been Jerry Brown's classmate at Yale Law School. A native New Yorker, Kline moved to California after law school with Brown. In 1965 and 1966 Kline and Brown worked together as law clerks to justices of the California Supreme Court in San Francisco.

When Kline started a "public interest" law firm (Kline-Gnaisda Public Advocates, Inc.) in San Francisco, Paul Halvonik joined him as a partner.

From 1968 to 1972, Halvonik served as Northern California Director of the American Civil Liberties Union (ACLU). He was also involved in litigation which banned the death penalty in California, and a legal action which invalidated residency requirements for voting in California elections. The latter issue was brought while Jerry Brown, then Secretary of State of California, was pressing for postcard voter registration.

When Brown was elected governor, he turned to his pal Kline for help in selecting his staff appointments and filling other positions. One of the first appointments was Paul N. Halvonik, who was made one of the top six members of the Brown administration. Halvonik served as Assistant to the Governor for Legislative Affairs in 1975.

In 1976, after Halvonik became bored with the staff job, Brown named him State Public Defender — the first person to hold that position. Even though the appointment required Senate confirmation, Brown never submitted his nomination to the State Senate. Instead, Halvonik was kept in that position for two years, unconfirmed, as the "acting" defender. Brown gave the excuse that he had intended to move Halvonik up to a judgeship all along.[8]

After 15 years of close association with Jerry Brown, Paul Halvonik learned there are no "friends" in politics — at least not when you become an embarrassing liability to Jerry Brown's ambitions. But Halvonik was not to be outdone by Brown in a test of loyalty — or lack of it. Caught red-handed, Paul Halvonik did the sensible thing — he blamed his wife, Deborah.[9]

Judge Halvonik pled not guilty to the Oakland drug charges. His wife also pled innocent, but asked to be placed in a drug rehabilitation program in order to avoid standing trial.[10]

During the Oakland police investigation, both Halvoniks claimed the drugs belonged to Deborah. Both also made some interesting, contradictions and damning statements. Deborah admitted that she had seen her husband use marijuana many times. When asked if that was more than 100 times, she replied: "I just don't know." Use of pot was so common in their household, she said, that it just didn't provoke comment. "It's like asking how many times in the last eight years have you washed your hands." [11]

Judge Halvonik also admitted to using marijuana, including as recently as September 10, 1979, just ten days before the raid, while he was at Lake Tahoe.[12] In his testimony before Municipal Court Judge Ken Kawaichi at a preliminary hearing, Paul Halvonik said that pot smoking "would not strike me as being a greater concern than serving a 19-year-old (individual) wine with dinner."[13]

Reporter Maitland Zane interviewed some of Judge Paul Halvonik's former associates in the State Public Defender's office. Zane reported that one of those coworkers told him that she had seen Halvonik smoking marijuana at several parties. She added, "He lived in a society that thought pot shouldn't be against the law."[14]

The Halvoniks were able to reach a plea-bargain arrangement with the Alameda County District Attorney's Office. Deborah pled guilty to possession of more than one ounce of marijuana, was given a suspended jail sentence, and was fined $500. Judge Paul N. Halvonik pled "no contest" to a misdemeanor charge of marijuana possession, was given a six month suspended jail sentence, was placed on probation, and resigned his judgeship.

As former-Judge Halvonik's critics said at the time, the issue wasn't just about a private individual casually abusing drugs. As a Judge, Halvonik was flouting the laws. He was also prejudiced and in a conflict of interest when drug abuse cases came before his court. More generally, he was ruling on important and complex legal issues which required careful and strenuous intellectual effort and mental clarity which heavy use of marijuana could well affect.

CHAPTER TWO

WHAT ARE FRIENDS FOR, ANYWAY?

Fred Gabourie believes friends should help each other. Unfortunately, he went overboard, and became the subject of a fraud investigation. He was eventually indicted for conspiracy to prevent and to obstruct justice.

Gabourie is a former movie stuntman who was a defense attorney when appointed by Governor Jerry Brown to the Los Angeles Municipal Court bench in January of 1976.

Before his appointment to the judiciary, Gabourie had gained notoriety as one of the lawyers who helped negotiate an end to the violent occupation of Wounded Knee, South Dakota in 1973 by radical Indian activist Dennis Banks and his followers. Banks and Gabourie began a friendship then that has proven mutually supportive.[1]

During the Wounded Knee episode, Banks and his cohorts in the American Indian Movement (AIM) occupied the Custer County Courthouse; the Chamber of Commerce building was fire-bombed; two police cars were overturned, looted, and burned; and seven police officers received injuries requiring hospitalization.[2]

As a result of that incident, Dennis Banks was found guilty of assault with a deadly weapon by a South Dakota jury. Two days before he was to be sentenced, Banks fled to California. South Dakota requested extradition of Banks from Governor Jerry Brown. After nearly a year of waiting, South Dakota filed suit to force Brown to extradite Banks.[3]

The California Supreme Court ruled that Brown could grant asylum, but had to take some formal action on the South Dakota request. Brown granted Banks asylum on April 20, 1978. Following the Supreme Court decision, it was learned that at the time the case was being heard by the California Supreme Court, Bank's attorney, Karen Spelke, was also employed on the staff of California Supreme Court Justice Wiley Manuel (also a Jerry Brown appointee).[4]

Banks went on to form Deqanowidah-Quetzalcoatl University (D-Q U) on abandoned federal property outside Davis, California. Gabourie became an attorney in California.

Through his law practice, Gabourie became involved with several investment schemes. One was with a man named Alfred J. Cusino. Cusino claimed to be an inventor who had a device to solve the smog problem, and another he called an "electrical energy multiplier."[5]

Gabourie was Cusino's lawyer. Connie Cox, Cusino's long time bookkeeper testified before a federal grand jury in San Francisco that Gabourie was also Cusino's "chief honcho and ringleader."[6]

Gabourie helped Cusino set up several corporations to finance and market his devices. According to Connie Cox, she testified that "no move was to be made in these corporations without Fred Gabourie's approval. I testified that when Gabourie talked, Al Cusino jumped." She also stated that "Cusino took all his instructions from Fred Gabourie until the day I left in May, 1977." (A year and a half after Gabourie was named to the judiciary.)[7]

In order to raise money for his enterprises, Al Cusino held meetings with unwary potential investors. One meeting was held at a hotel in Santa Rosa, California on November 9, 1975. About 100 people attended. Cusino introduced the investors to Fred W. Gabourie who would, he said, "set the right course" for the business. Cusino described Gabourie as "the closest man to God that I can find."[8]

A tape recording made at the meeting at the El Rancho Tropicana Hotel shows Gabourie detailing the status of Cusino's corporations to the investors. Not mentioned by Gabourie on those tapes was that the California Department of Corporations had ordered Cusino to stop the selling of stock in the state. The department's records show that a copy of the order was sent to Gabourie.[9]

Gabourie advised the investors who held promissory notes from Cusino's companies that the "safest way to go" was to convert the notes to shares in a new Cusino controlled general partnership. That conversion, Gabourie claimed would give the investors "tax advantages."[10]

Gabourie also told his audience that two companies had contacted him about buying the Cusino "inventions." There was, Gabourie said to the investors, "a time in my office in which we discussed the possible sale of this machine to a

Japanese corporation called Multi-National, Inc. It's out of Inglewood." That firm, Gabourie claimed, was an "adjunct corporation of Toyota or one of the Japanese firms — Nissan Motors if you will."[11] (Nissan at the time was the maker of Datsun, not Toyota.)

Gabourie also said that a firm called "Crosby Corporation" or "Crosby Enterprises" had also made an offer, but it was unacceptable.

An investigation by *Los Angeles Herald Examiner* reporters could find no such companies as Gabourie has named.[12]

Cusino was eventually charged with both state and federal crimes in relation to his stock sales. He was convicted and sentenced to both state and federal prison and ordered to repay millions to the investors.[13]

During the federal investigations, Cusino told Federal Magistrate Richard Goldsmith that only Gabourie could answer all the questions.[14]

According to Connie Cox, Gabourie was well paid for his services. Among the payments to Gabourie from Cusino, she said, were a check for $1,000, cash totaling over $5,000, and a new Lincoln Mark IV worth $14,000 — all given to Gabourie in October of 1975.[15]

Cox also said that Gabourie received as much as $15,000 as late as May, 1977 — a year and a half after Gabourie had become a judge.[16]

There is additional evidence that Gabourie was financially tied to Cusino after becoming a judge. Gabourie had hired patent attorney Dan Haycock to file a patent claim for Cusino. Haycock and the judge participated in a meeting in North Hollywood on February 28, 1976 — after Gabourie's judicial appointment. Haycock sent Gabourie a bill for the meeting.[17]

Gabourie apparently also used his connections with Dennis Banks, of D-Q U, for a curious arrangement. Cusino had told investors that his devices were going to be tested by D-Q U. Gabourie was a chancellor of that college.[18]

The Securities and Exchange Commission found that Cusino's books claimed $417,000 from Multi-Power Corp. — one of Cusino's companies — had been spent for various activities and improvements at D-Q U. The SEC, however, could only find about $3,000 worth of actual work done on the campus with those funds.[19] The Cusino inventions were never tested at the college.

According to Dennis Banks, Cusino might have spent as much as $25,000 in repairs, heavy equipment rental, and construction of a reservoir on the campus. But, Banks said, "There was not that much investment — $400,000."[20]

Banks, a friend of both Gabourie and Governor Brown, said he and Cusino "became very close friends. He never did us any harm. There's a lot of white people that have tried to destroy us here at D-Q. He (Cusino) never came here to screw us."[21]

When he was talking about people trying to destroy D-Q, Banks might have been referring to federal Department of Education auditors who visited the campus. In 1982 the "university" was receiving $489,000 in tax dollars. The campus was a deserted Army base on loan to the two-year D-Q University. To qualify for the assistance, the school was supposed to have 200 students. D-Q U records claimed only 86 students, and auditors had been able to locate only a few dozen of those. In one class there were supposedly 15 students. The auditors found none — and no teacher.[22] But then only a prejudiced person would question the integrity of Dennis Banks and D-Q U.

In order to successfully prosecute stock fraud, or any other crime, it must be shown beyond a reasonable doubt that the defendant knowingly committed the crime. No one can be forced to testify against himself. Nor may prosecutors force disclosure of information from a confidential client-attorney relationship.

Gabourie was not been charged in the stock fraud cases. His former client, Al Cusino, was sentenced to prison.

The Cusino affair was not the only one in which Fred Gabourie was implicated. In February 1980, securities fraud charges were filed in Colorado by the Arapahoe County District Attorney against two Malibu, California promoters — Jerry Schafer and Harry Ira Geller.

The two men had proposed a combined motion picture and amusement park project based on a science fiction theme. Originally they had looked for locations for the project in Canada, but decided instead to seek a site 13 miles from Denver.[23]

When they first concocted their plan, Schafer and Geller went through Judge Gabourie for a Canadian business contact. Gabourie and Schafer had both been stuntmen for the movies and had worked together.[24] Schafer had also been a

Jerry Brown contributor as early as 1968.

Gabourie put Schafer and Geller in touch with a Toronto businessman, Harold "Hal" Halpenny. Schafer and Halpenny met at a hotel by the Los Angeles International Airport in late 1979. At that meeting Schafer gave Halpenny a letter of intent concerning his project, and the letter was witnessed by Judge Gabourie.[25]

Judge Gabourie knew Halpenny through his nephew, Fred Patrick "Freddie" Gabourie. Freddie was working for Halpenny as part of a work release program from a Canadian jail. Freddie had been sentenced to seven years in prison for serving as a leader in a "Granny fraud" scheme which preyed on elderly people. Sixteen of his accomplices were also convicted by Canadian courts. Freddie was released in 1979, after serving only two years, in order to work for Halpenny. Halpenny assigned Freddie the task of examining possible Canadian sites for Schafer and Geller's science fiction project.[26]

On December 3, 1979, two weeks before Schafer and Geller officially announced that they had selected the Denver area for their project, nephew Freddie Gabourie was found dead in a Toronto motel. The cause of the death was variously reported as natural causes or possible suicide.[27]

Because Freddie had a criminal record, Canadian police sent intelligence officers to his funeral. Those officers reported that the wake was a virtual "who's who of the Toronto crime world."[28] Geller and Schafer were not implicated in Freddie Gabourie's death.[29]

Schafer and Geller continued promoting the Colorado site for their sci-fi movie and theme park. Schafer and Geller had apparently convinced respected names in the science fiction entertainment field, and even some former athletic heroes, to invest in and to become involved in the project.[30]

Part of their selling job included a press conference at which they announced that the movie alone would cost over $50 million — making it the most expensive film in history. The movie, named "Lord of Light," would leave elaborate sets to become the core of the sci-fi amusement park. The movie and 1,000 acre park, the promoters said, would be financed by sales of land in an adjacent 10,000 acre industrial park.[31]

The Schafer/Geller team claimed at their press conference that while the project was starting with just half a million in cash, they had an irrevocable letter of credit from the Royal Bank of Canada. An investigation by the *Los Angeles Times*, however, learned that such credit had never been given by that bank. The investigators found out, in fact, that Schafer had filed for bankruptcy in a federal court in Los Angeles just 19 months earlier.[32]

Schafer pled Nolo Contendere to securities fraud and was sentenced on September 10, 1980 to five years probation and ordered to make total restitution. Charges against Geller were dismissed.

In both of the securities fraud cases, Judge Fred Gabourie may only have been guilty of involving himself in helping friends whose intentions were less than honorable — or whose plans were at least somewhat shaky. He was never indicted in either case. Yet his downfall was caused by another incident of doing a little favor for friends. On January 14, 1980, Judge Gabourie was indicted along with three others for conspiracy to pervert or obstruct justice and for removal and altering of government documents.[33]

Indicted with Gabourie were two Hollywood attorneys, Harry Weiss and his nephew Sammy Weiss. Gabourie, of course, was a friend and appointee of Governor Jerry Brown. The Weisses were also Jerry's friends — to the tune of $1,657 in donations to Jerry's primary election campaign in early 1978 and $6,150 in donations to Brown's general election campaign in November 1978.[34]

In October 1978, about the same time the Weisses were giving their substantial contributions to Brown's re-election campaign, Judge Gabourie took a temporary assignment with the West Los Angeles Municipal Court to fill in for a vacationing judge. Gabourie usually sat on the Municipal Court bench in the Van Nuys area.

Just prior to Gabourie beginning his temporary stint with the West Los Angeles court, the Weisses had taken the cases of two clients facing drunk driving charges in that court. On September 26, 1978 Sammy Weiss told one of the two clients that he didn't have to show up for a scheduled hearing.[35] At about the same time the other client was told by Henry Weiss that his case was being delayed because, "Well, we just have to wait to see the friendly judge and the friendly clerk."[36]

In the first case, a warrant was issued for the arrest of the client for not appearing at his hearing. One of Gabourie's early actions after taking up his temporary duties on the West Los Angeles court was to withdraw the arrest warrant.[37] In October 1978 that client was told that his case had been "taken care of" and that he would only have to pay a $350 fine. On December 14, 1978 the client paid the fine to the Weiss law firm. The client was told that the case was settled on the terms that he wanted. The case, however, was actually still pending in December and for several months after.[38]

In the second case, Harry Weiss had, according to the indictment of the Los Angeles Grand Jury, removed a case file from the court room of Judge Roy M. Corstairs on October 10, 1978, and seventeen days later gave it to Judge Gabourie and his clerk Joseph L. Eggleston.

The judge and the clerk allegedly altered the docketing record to falsely show that the case had not been in the earlier court.[39]

On October 27, 1978 Judge Gabourie, in an extremely unusual procedure, transferred the two cases from the West Los Angeles court back with him to his regular assignment with the Van Nuys court. Hearings on the cases were also postponed to June 6, 1980 and July 13, 1980.[40]

According to the Los Angeles District Attorney's Office, the cases were apparently postponed so that the clients would not be found guilty of drunk driving twice within a five year period. Two such convictions in that time frame meant the loss of a driver's license and 48 hours in jail.[41]

CHAPTER THREE

MORE FRIENDS

A key issue in the case against Gabourie was his handling of Los Angeles Municipal Court files. Specifically, files on two drunk driving cases vanished from the West Los Angeles Municipal Court Chambers of Judge Gabourie.

Since local court procedure was an issue, an out of county judge was obtained to hold the preliminary hearing. The judge selected to hear the case was Judge Joanna Herald from Orange County. A Jerry Brown appointee, incidentally, Judge Herald enjoyed a very good reputation as a no-nonsense judge who started her court calendar on time and kept it moving.

The Weisses objected to Judge Herald's appointment and filed an affidavit with the court to remove her from the case. The California Judicial Council, with Chief Rose Bird concurring, then appointed Los Angeles Superior Court Judge Gilbert Alston to act as the preliminary hearing judge in the Municipal Court proceedings. Presumably the idea behind Alston's appointment was to have the case heard by someone in the area who was not part of the Los Angeles Municipal Court system.[1] However, in making this appointment, the Judicial Council overlooked a few facts. First, Alston had been a Los Angeles Municipal Court judge prior to his appointment to the Superior Court. Second, he had served on the Municipal Court at the same time as Gabourie. In short, the Judicial Council may as well have selected a sitting Los Angeles Municipal Court Judge.[2]

The Los Angeles District Attorney's Office on January 11, 1982 filed a motion alleging that Alston should be disqualified from hearing the case due to his bias or prejudice.

Since the case dealt with disqualifying a pro tem Los Angeles Court Judge, the motion to disqualify was transferred to an out of county judge. Orange County Superior Court Judge Harold Robert E. Rickles was assigned by the Judicial

Council to hear the arguments.[3]

The Los Angeles District Attorney's Office argued that Alston was biased for the following reasons:

1) Alston and defendant Weiss were long-time friends;

2) Harry Weiss' attorney, Robert L. Shapiro, was a campaign contributor to Judge Alston's "Committee to Re-Elect Judge Gilbert C. Alston";

3) Alston had also received a campaign contribution from defendant Sammy M. Weiss;

4) Both Alston and Gabourie had been assigned to hear criminal matters in the same court building in 1977;

5) Judge Alston had in one previous case accused the Deputy District Attorney prosecuting the Gabourie case of racism;

6) That Judge Alston was biased against law enforcement officers based on a drunk driving investigation of Alston's wife. Specifically, it was "alleged by the investigating officers that Judge Alston involved himself in the investigation of the incident with the result that the officers were unable to interview his wife or perform any type of tests that may have lead to the ascertainment of her 'blood-alcohol' level."[4]

Judge Alston denied saying that he and Weiss were long-time friends. He did admit to using "rather colorful language" in court that was "admittedly in bad taste" to a Deputy District Attorney, Brent Riggs. He denied even knowing if Shapiro or Weiss were campaign contributors. He also denied recalling any meeting with Gabourie when they worked in the same building, but acknowledged that "it is indisputable that there must have been many occasions on which Judges Alston and Gabourie met in the hallways concerning court business..." Alston stated he had "no recollection whatsoever" of having accused Deputy District Attorney Michael Brenner of racism.[5]

On January 27, Judge Rickles denied the District Attorney's motion without bothering to hold a hearing on the fact or arguments of either side.[6] For Judge Rickles to make such a summary ruling, he had to find not only a lack of real bias but an absence of even an appearance of bias.

Judge Rickles should have re-read the remarks of former Justice Clark in *Wood v. City Civil Service Commission* (1975): "Judicial power will not long endure if public respect and confidence is destroyed because judicial power is exercised in an unfair manner or appears to be exercised in an unfair manner."

Considering Judge Rickles attitude on bias, it probably would not have made any difference if the Los Angeles District Attorney's motion had also included the fact that Alston attended Judge Gabourie's fund raiser on March 24, 1980 at General Lee's restaurant in Los Angeles' Chinatown — after Gabourie had already been indicted! Nor would it have been important to Judge Rickles that the Los Angeles District Attorney's Pasadena Office regularly filed affidavits of bias against Judge Alston because they felt that he was hostile to law enforcement.

To understand why the District Attorney's Office felt that Alston was biased against law enforcement we have only to look at two of the cases cited in the motion which Judge Rickles dismissed.

First, on July 13, 1977, a car driven by Alston's wife reportedly failed to stop at a stop sign at Henrietta Street and Lincoln Avenue in Altadena and struck another car causing heavy damage to both cars and "visible injuries" to the driver of the second car.[7]

When Altadena Sheriff's Deputy Fred Browning arrived Mrs. Alston was phoning her husband. Browning said he "observed her eyes to be red and watery, her speech to be slurred and smelled a strong odor of an alcoholic beverage emitting from her breath." Mrs. Alston then told Deputy Browning that she had a couple of glasses of wine about two hours before the accident.[8]

California Highway Patrol Officer Pat Morrow arrived on the scene and took charge of the investigation since the incident was under the Highway Patrol's jurisdiction. Moments later Judge Alston arrived accompanied by his court bailiff. The Judge reportedly asked that his wife be questioned no further until she could be seen by a doctor. Officer Morrow agreed.[9]

Judge Alston then phoned for another county marshal and a marshal's car to drive his wife to Huntington Memorial Hospital in Pasadena.[10]

Morrow, a rookie officer, later admitted that "the mere fact that he (Alston) was a judge had me intimidated." So Morrow called Highway Patrol Officer Robert Callahan and asked Callahan to accompany him. After checking with the hospital's medical staff and receiving their authorization to interview Mrs. Alston the officers headed for her room.[11]

Judge Alston stopped the officers outside the room and refused to let them enter to interview his wife. Morrow reportedly told Alston that they were investigating a crime, possible drunk driving.[12]

Judge Alston then reportedly said "Why don't you guys just wise up and get out of here."[13] Alston denies that he said it.

Morrow said that Alston blocked the door with his body and outstretched arms. Alston says that he merely stood in the doorway without outstretched arms.[14]

After again informing Alston that they were investigating a crime, Alston is alleged to have said, "If you guys step past me, you're both going to wind up with some days off." Alston recalls warning them that they could face days off if they failed to get a superior officer to the scene.[15]

At this point, California Highway Patrol Sergeant Miller arrived. Then Mrs. Alston's attorney, Ray Fountain showed up. Sgt. Miller took charge of the case and discussed it with Mr. Fountain. No further effort was made by any of the California Highway Patrol Officers to talk with Mrs. Alston and she was never given a sobriety test. In fact, the Highway Patrol never did interview the suspect, Mrs. Alston.[16]

The California Highway Patrol wrote the report and shipped it to the Pasadena District Attorney's Office. Deputy District Attorney Doug Bruce was assigned to the case.[17]

Judge Alston called the District Attorney's Office and asked that another deputy be assigned to the case. It seems that Alston had ordered Bruce out of his courtroom in an unrelated case two weeks earlier and Alston felt that Bruce might be biased. The case was reassigned to Deputy District Attorney Charles Benson. However, Officers Morrow and Browning, and Deputy District Attorney Bruce were all interviewed by the Star-News and called for an investigation of Judge Alston for obstructing a peace officer in his investigation.[18]

Eventually, the Special Investigations Division of the Los Angeles County District Attorney's Office investigated the matter and considered filing criminal charges against Judge Alston but did not do so.

The second case cited in the motion to remove Alston was *People v. Debby Sue Vanella*.

On July 24, 1979, two Burbank undercover officers (Rombach and Santos) arranged to buy $5,000 in cocaine from a Richard Novikoff. Debby Sue Vanella arrived to deliver the cocaine but then attempted to exit the driveway without making delivery. Another Burbank officer, D'Amicis, drove his car in front of the driveway to block her exit and she backed into him. Officer Rombach approached Vanella's car and asked Officer Brown "Where is the dope?" At that, Vanella produced 11 grams of cocaine from her pocket. In court, Vanella was represented by Harry Weiss.[19]

Weiss filed an affidavit of prejudice against Judge Richard Torres who had been given the case and had consistently denied various defense motions. The case was reassigned to Judge Alston.[20]

During the trial, the defense did not call any witnesses nor offer any defense. But after Sgt. Brown testified, Weiss requested a dismissal and Judge Alston dismissed the charges. Judge Alston based his dismissal on the grounds that Officer Rombach's testimony (as to what he heard Novikoff say in a series of phone calls during which Romback was present) was hearsay.[21] When the prosecutor, Brent Riggs, and Sgt. Brown asked the judge to explain his ruling, Alston said that the case was "the shittiest investigation I have ever seen. If you don't know how to do your job, get a job as a plumber, the pay is better. You deliberately rammed the lady's car because she's backing out of a driveway and then you arrest her. You didn't even have probable cause to detain her." Alston then went on to suggest that the Deputy District Attorney was involved in this "wrongdoing."[22]

Later, in the Judge's chambers, Alston again accused the officers of running their car into Vanella's: "They have no business ramming her car. She could have been killed."[23]

Riggs pointed out that Vanella had hit the officer's car trying to escape and that a prior judge — Torres — had already ruled for the prosecution on that point.[24]

Alston then charged that the police could have planted the dope on Vanella![25]

The last insight which Riggs gives us is that Alston based his decision "upon a case in a bound volume of approximately 1930's vintage, which the court (Alston) apparently already had open before it on the bench before the evidence was even offered..."[26]

Burbank Police Chief James L. Shaffer felt that Judge Alston's attacks on his officers and, indeed, on his whole department were wrong. Further, Shaffer viewed Alston's actions as an attack upon the two judges who had heard the case before Alston had it (C. Bernard Kaufman who handled the preliminary hearing and Ricardo A. Torres, the first trial judge).[27]

Shaffer found that Alston was "unprofessional" and "totally biased against law enforcement." Shaffer thought that he knew exactly what to do: he filed a complaint with the Commission on Judicial Performance on April 9, 1981.[28]

On May 15, 1981, Los Angeles County Supervisor Mike Antonovich joined in the call for an investigation.[29]

On June 17, 1981, Mr. Jack Frankel of the Commission on Judicial Performance advised Chief Shaffer that "It was the decision of the Commission not to proceed further with the matter."[30]

If these two cases don't give you a good idea of what Alston thought of the criminal justice system, then you only have to read what he has said himself.

"State prison is no place for a young person, he (Alston) said. Even at the age of 18, they're still impressionable."[31]

In 1981, a young woman was kidnapped, robbed, and subjected to multiple rapes (and worse). The ordeal only ended when police arrived on the scene. Alston observed that the girl "was practically unscathed by what otherwise would have been a terrifying experience..." He then sentenced the convicted defendants to serve minimum prison terms of 21 and 22 years rather than the 133 and 131 years that he could have. Alston said that the longer sentences would be viewed as cruel and unusual punishment. Besides, he said, a judge "should make the sentence fit the crime and the defendant."[32]

Alston had explained his sentencing philosophy by saying, "I'm not a big believer in jail because it doesn't do anything for anyone."[33]

An appointee of Governor Jerry Brown, Alston is a liberal Democrat who the Los Angeles Bar Association has rated "well qualified."

But back to the Gabourie case, on January 27, 1982 Judge Rickles found Alston to be without even the appearance of bias. On March 11, 1982, Judge Alston, back on the case, dismissed all charges against Gabourie and his three codefendants.

In his decision, Alston failed to explain away any of the evidence in the case. He could not. So, he chose to ignore it. The disappearance of two court case files from one court and their reappearance in Judge Gabourie's court is unexplained. What the Weisses did with one of their clients' "fines" will, apparently, remain a secret of the Weisses. The taped conversations between a Weiss client and one of the Weisses concerning getting the client's case into the hands of a favorable judge will not be investigated by the courts. These, and many other questions about this case will never be answered.[34]

Probably afraid of the controversy that his decision would cause, Judge Alston issued a controversial (and probably unconstitutional) gag order. Alston ordered "all of the attorneys, defendants, and their staff" not to discuss the case. This was after he had decided the case.[35]

When questioned about the gag order — or the case — Alston would merely cite his own order and say that he could not "discuss the case. I'd be in violation of my own order if I did that."

With the deck already stacked against them, the District Attorney's Office fought to appeal Alston's decision.

On June 4, 1982, Orange County Superior Court Judge James Turner upheld Judge Alston's decision.[36]

CHAPTER FOUR

CONTEMPT OF COURT

Divorce is never pleasant, and it's always hard to deal with. Public officials, including judges, aren't immune to the ravages of failed marriages. The question, however, is how they deal with it.

Judges are supposed to uphold the law. As the California Code of Judicial Conduct states:

> "A judge should respect and comply with the law and should conduct himself at all times in a manner that promotes public confidence in the integrity and impartiality of the judiciary." (Cal. Code of Jud. Cond. p. 197)

It is because judges represent the law itself that we hold them to the highest standards of conduct. And that is why it is so shocking to most citizens when a judge is seen to be flouting the law.

We also expect judges to be responsible people. The shock of a judge ignoring the law is compounded when he is also ignoring his responsibility to his family — and in such a serious manner as to be found guilty of contempt of court.

One California judge who found himself in such a situation was Robert D. Fratianne, a judge of the Los Angeles County Superior Court (Van Nuys District). Judge Fratianne was appointed by Governor Brown on October 17, 1978.

Judge Fratianne and his wife Virginia have five children. Their third child is Linda Fratianne, a two-time world figure skating champion and an Olympic silver medalist.

While Robert Fratianne was still an attorney, and while Linda was learning skating under the direction of her mother, the Fratiannes began drifting apart. Virginia spent most of her time with her daughter, while Robert spent his with his law practice. As too often happens in such situations, the

Fratianne marriage ended in divorce in January of 1981.

In the divorce settlement, Judge Fratianne was ordered to pay $600 per month in alimony and $300 a month in child support for a 14 year old son living with Virginia. At the time the judge was making $62,760 a year from his judicial salary — $5,230 per month.[1]

Despite his income, and the court order, the judge fell seriously behind in the payments. On August 31, 1981, Judge Fratianne was brought before Judge James L. Smith on contempt of court charges for failing to pay child support and alimony. Fratianne argued that he had not been properly served the notice of the court order to make the payments, so Judge Smith had to dismiss the contempt charges.[2]

Fratianne also argued that he could not afford to make the payments. (He would, of course, have been left with only $4,330 a month to live on.) While dismissing the contempt charges, Judge Smith found that Fratianne did have the ability to comply with the payment order. Smith stated: "I feel myself getting sick if this case comes back. It was a tough situation because it was a judge charged with contempt."[3]

The case did come back. In September of 1981, Fratianne was again charged with contempt of court. At the time he was more than $5,390 behind in the court-ordered payments — out of $8,370 he owed.

The judge's paychecks from Los Angeles County were garnished after the hearing on the first contempt charges, following his continued failure to make the monthly payments.[4]

Again Judge Fratianne escaped the contempt charges. This time by agreeing in mid-November 1981 to pay the amounts overdue and to make the regular monthly payments.[5]

While Judge Fratianne's situation was serious, it was mild compared to that of another Brown appointee.

In March of 1978, Governor Brown appointed John J. Miller to be an Associate Justice of the First District Court of Appeal. Miller had been an Assemblyman for six years — 1971 through 1977 — representing a district in the Oakland area.

It is obvious from Miller's voting record in the California State Assembly that Jerry Brown wasn't looking for a tough law-and-order judge when he appointed Miller to the bench. During his time in the Assembly, Miller had one of the worst voting records in the eyes of "pro-law and order" organizations. Three groups, the California Peace Officers' Association, the California District Attorneys' and the California Sheriffs' Association, rated state legislators on key issues important to those groups. Miller, in his six years in the Assembly, had voted with those groups only 9 times. He voted against them 61 times. And he failed to vote on 21 key law and order issues.[6]

When Miller's appointment was announced, even the usually passive California State Bar Association was concerned. The Bar rarely takes any action to oppose a judicial appointment. In Miller's case, however, the group made the unusual request to meet with the Governor to discuss their concerns about Miller's qualifications - and to discuss several substantial complaints which the Bar said had been filed against Miller.[7]

The Board of Governors of the California State Bar Association had reviewed eleven disciplinary complaints against Miller, prior to his appointment as a judge. The Bar decided to give Miller the benefit of the doubt and declared that he was "qualified" for the post. Miller was confirmed to the judgeship on December 26, 1978.

When Miller was an Assemblyman his Administrative Aide was Elihu Harris. When Miller became a judge, Harris succeeded Miller as Assemblyman. Harris then hired Miller's wife Joyce to be his Administrative Aide.[8] Unfortunately, the story doesn't end there.

Just one month after his confirmation to the appellate bench, Justice Miller and his wife were separated. Their year-old daughter went with Mrs. Miller.[9] Their two teenage sons stayed with the judge.[10]

The Millers went through a bitter divorce. In their settlement the judge agreed to pay alimony of $600 per month, and child support of $300 per month. But by January of 1980 he was already $5,300 behind. At the time the judge was earning over $5,400 per month from his judicial salary.[11]

The judge was ordered to appear in court for a contempt hearing on his failure to pay. The contempt charges were dropped when he agreed to catch up on the over-due amounts and gave his ex-wife a check for $1,000.[12] That check cleared the bank, but a second check to her attorney to pay for her legal expenses (which he had also been ordered to pay) bounced.[13]

In February 1980 the judge was again ordered back into court for a contempt hearing for failure to make the court-ordered payments. By then Miller was $6,950 behind, and half his state salary had been garnished.[14]

In the hearing Justice Miller was represented by John George, a Democrat Alameda County Supervisor. Mrs. Miller was represented by a Beverly Hills attorney, Daniel Jaffe. According to Jaffe, Mrs. Miller couldn't get a lawyer in the San Francisco Bay Area to represent her because local attorneys didn't relish the idea of offending an appellate judge.[15]

The hearing was settled in a closed meeting in the chambers of Judge Michael Ballachey. It resulted in a reduction of the monthly payments — to $700 per month — and an agreement by Justice Miller to pay the delinquent amount in payments of $200 per month. Again Miller had escaped contempt charges.[16]

According to Mrs. Miller's attorney, Daniel Jaffe, the hearings "no doubt — make that probably — saved Justice Miller from being held in contempt of court, and from being jailed."[17] That would have been an unsettling end to a bad story. Unfortunately, it wasn't.

Despite the close call, Miller again failed to keep the divorce settlement. In July of 1980, he was hauled back into the court for another contempt hearing. By then the amount he owed had grown to $8,300.[18]

In the hearing, Judge Lyle Cook of the Alameda Superior Court found that "The record shows he (Justice Miller) did have the money in hand to pay the support had he so wished." Cook found Miller guilty of contempt of court for failure to pay child support. Miller was ordered to sell his "$205,000 home in Berkeley and to pay off his debts." Sentencing for the contempt charge was delayed to give Miller another chance to pay.[19]

In all, Miller was charged twenty-two times with contempt of court. He was found guilty of contempt, and ordered to sell his home to pay his legal debts.

CHAPTER FIVE

THE LAW AND THE PROPHET

Judges have an awesome responsibility. They hold both the safety of the community and the future of each defendant in their hands. Most judges, recognizing this power and their own human failings, approach their duties with the cautious attitude called judicial temperament.

Unfortunately, there are others who allow that power to swell their egos and affect their judgment. Few, however, assume that they have been anointed by God as His infallible instruments: a view apparently sincerely held by Judge Hugh Wesley Goodwin.

Goodwin was appointed by Governor Jerry Brown to the Fresno Municipal Court on January 29, 1976. Prior to that Goodwin had been an Assistant Public Defender in Fresno County for nine years. He had previously been a member of the Fresno City Council and the Fresno County Board of Supervisors.

When Goodwin was sworn in to his office as a judge, he did not follow the tradition of a small, dignified, formal ceremony. Instead he planned a celebration in the Fresno Municipal Auditorium with over 300 invited guests, mostly from his church, and a program that would "...take a couple of hours," including singing by the choir of his church. As Goodwin remarked, the ceremony was to celebrate that "... the appointment was made by God, and not by the Governor."[1]

Goodwin was, and is, a sincerely religious man. But his view of religion, public office, and his own capabilities resulted in a strange way of administering justice.

In a letter published in the *Fresno Bee* on December 7, 1978, Judge Goodwin wrote, "To say that they (public officials) don't claim infallibility for the decisions they make may sound humble before men but it doesn't sound that way to God. God promises just that — infallibility — for every decision He makes through you..."

Goodwin had already declared his appointment to the bench to be an act of God. Apparently he also believed that as God's anointed justice, his decisions were infallible. Among those decisions which he believed were inspired, there were over 200 — in the less than three years he served as a judge — in which he gave suspended sentences and probation instead of fines and jail if those convicted agreed to attend church.[2] Many of those were Traffic Court cases, and there is nothing wrong with recommending that people go to church and mend their ways. The effect of some of Goodwin's actions, however, was to release not just speeders, but also violent law-breakers without punishment.

In one particular case, a seventeen year-old young man, Samuel Allen Alford, pled guilty to the forcible statutory rape of a fourteen year old girl in 1976.[3] Alford already had a seven year record of juvenile delinquency.[4] But instead of sending the violent criminal to a California Youth Authority prison, Judge Goodwin decided to give him probation - provided that he go to church and mind his mother.

Instead of protecting the community from a violent person, Goodwin had concluded that releasing him would change the young man's heart. Unfortunately, it didn't.

As could be expected, Alford failed to attend church. His probation officer discovered that fact several months later and had Alford arrested for violating his probation. Alford was brought before another Judge who sentenced him to a year at the California Youth Authority prison in Stockton.[5]

Alford's state-provided lawyer, however, learned of the church attendance condition of probation and filed a Writ of Habeas Corpus. The lawyer argued that church attendance as a condition of probation was a violation of religious freedom. In Fresno, Superior Court Judge Hollis G. Best ruled that the condition for probation was a violation of religious freedom. Judge Best ruled that Alford's lawyer's arguments were legally right, and reluctantly released Alford.

A year later, on September 30, 1977, Samuel Alford attacked another young girl — raped her, and cut her with a broken bottle. He was found guilty of that crime on June 21, 1978 and sentenced to four years in State Prison. The judge in that case, William K. Kessler of Fresno Superior Court, stated while sentencing Alford that "He has not said anything about remorse or mitigating circumstances, and in light of that I have to see Mr. Alford as a man who feels using force to accomplish sexual desires is acceptable as a way of life."[6]

A young girl had suffered a brutal assault and rape because Judge Goodwin has been blind to the threat posed by Alford to the community, and had relied instead on his self-assumed infallibility to change Alford with a lenient, illegal and unenforceable probation.

When asked by a probation officer why he gave such a probation, Goodwin replied: "The Lord made me do it."[7] That wasn't good enough for the California Commission on Judicial Performance. That official body investigated Goodwin's sentencing and reprimanded him for "conduct prejudicial to the administration of justice that brings the judicial office into disrepute and with willful misconduct in office."[8]

To complaints that he was violating separation of church and state, Goodwin replied that "Three quarters of the (U.S.) Constitution should rewritten, not only the doctrine of separating church and state... Our forefathers really flubbed it."[9]

When his fellow Municipal Court Judge, James V. Paige, challenged Goodwin's practices, Goodwin, in a rare unchristian tirade, publicly attacked Paige as being "stupid, guilty of abuse of discretion," and "out of his mind."[10] That's the kind of tough talk we might expect a judge to use in pronouncing sentence on a hardened young criminal.

In violation of the California Code of Judicial Conduct he also publicly endorsed a candidate for public office - Joel Crosby, who successfully sought a seat on the Fresno City Council in June, 1977. Goodwin was reprimanded by the California Commission on Judicial Performance for that endorsement.[11] Goodwin's response to that charge was a frank admission that, "We get numerous requests from Sacramento to support certain things and the basis of these requests always says something to the effect of 'remember who appointed you. To respond secretly and not openly is a deceit upon the people."[12]

On February 4, 1978, Judge Goodwin announced that he would run for the Democratic nomination for Governor as a write-in candidate. In his announcement, Goodwin declared: "Christ has again honored me. He has chosen me as His candidate for Governor in the November elections." He said, "The only question they (the voters) have to decide is, are they going to vote with God or without God."[13]

At the same time as his race for Governor, Goodwin

was up for re-election to his Municipal Court judgeship. In California, while the Governor appoints judges, the voters eventually have the opportunity to reelect or replace them. In the election on June 6, 1978, the voters of Fresno considered the evidence on Judge Goodwin's approach to justice and returned their verdict. They replaced Goodwin with Carl P. Evans — by a landslide margin of 59% to 41%.[14]

Judge Goodwin was returned to the private practice of law... and religion.

CHAPTER SIX

THE GANG'S ALL HERE

While Fresno Municipal Court Judge Goodwin ran into problems by improperly mixing his self-professed relationship with the Lord into his judicial duties, one of his colleagues in the Fresno court gained notoriety for some less desirable relationships.

Lenore Schreiber was an intelligent and aggressive lawyer with the Fresno County Public Defender's office when Governor Jerry Brown appointed her a Judge of the Fresno County Municipal Court in January 1978. When she was sworn in on February 17, 1978 she became the first woman judge ever to serve on the Fresno court.

Prior to her appointment, several senior members of the Fresno County District Attorney's Office staff wrote a letter to Governor Brown's Legal Affairs Secretary, Anthony Kline, strongly objecting to the appointment. The letter was signed by the Chief Deputy District Attorney Terry Wolfe, by Deputy District Attorney Phil Officer (who specialized in investigating crimes committed by prison spawned gangs), and by Deputy District Attorney Worth Bogel. They had never before objected to any judicial appointment.

In their letter they offered to provide specific details of their reasons for opposing Schreiber's appointment. Jerry Brown and his staff never bothered to contact them, never obtained the details offered, and went ahead with the appointment.[1]

What the Fresno D.A.'s staff had to say was that they had been investigating Schreiber for a year. The investigation was based on statements from several members of the Nuestra Familia and the EME/Mexican-Mafia gangs about her conduct while an attorney in the Public Defender's office.[2] Those statements included, according to Daral Kennedy of the D.A.'s office, comments that Schreiber may have participated in "active gang-type activities." Kennedy also reported that Schreiber allegedly visited members of the gangs in jail. She was their attorney, but, according to Kennedy, the visits were "unusual and not of a legal nature."[3]

In a report on Schreiber published on July 11, 1981, the *Fresno Bee* stated: "Her adversaries in the Fresno County District Attorney's Office say she is an unabashed sympathizer, even an accomplice, of killers and dope dealers." According to the *Fresno Bee* report, even "Her friends say that perhaps she allowed herself to get too close to her former clients."

One of those former clients was Daniel (Choco) Montellano, reputed to be part of the inner circle of the Mexican Mafia gang.[4] Montellano was also reputed to be a hit man for that gang. While he was Screiber's client, he was accused and in jail for murders in Fresno and Los Angeles. The Fresno murder was of Gilbert Roybal in February of 1977.[5] Roybal was shot with a sawed-off 20-gauge shotgun. The Los Angeles murder was of George (Poyo) Felix, also in February of 1977.

Even after her appointment to the California judiciary, Lenore Schreiber continued her relationship with Montellano. Records of the Los Angeles County jail showed that she visited Montellano five times after taking office as a judge.[6] Those visits occurred between February and May in 1978. According to Schreiber, those visits were necessary to "Introduce his new attorney and to establish trust." On two of those occasions, however, she claimed the new attorney "stood me up."[7] And so she met with Montellano alone. Subsequently, in November 1978, Schreiber admitted to visiting Montellano since May of that year in the Fresno County jail, to which he had been transferred.[8]

In October of 1978, while Montellano was out on bail, Schreiber — now a judge and not Montellano's attorney — met with him and, according to her, drove him to an appointment with a probation officer.[9] Investigative reporters for the *Los Angeles Times* reported that she had loaned her car to Montellano, which showed a closer relationship than would be normal even between an attorney and client.[10]

This unusual situation between a judge and a leader of a criminal gang led to an investigation by the California Council on Judicial Performance.[11] One of the judges on the Council, who told reporters he wished to remain anonymous, said that the relationship was "astonishing."[12] To Schreiber's claim that it was all an innocent attorney/client relationship, the judge said, "In the first place, judges are prohibited from practicing law. A judge cannot even be a member of the State Bar while he is on the bench. Therefore, you can't have an attorney-client relationship with anyone." The judge also said: "One of the cannons (of Judicial Conduct) states specifically that a judge should avoid impropriety and the appearance of impropriety."[13]

Schreiber herself stated that during her visits to Montellano she was in "no way attempting to practice law."[14]

Montellano eventually pled guilty to second-degree murder, and was sentenced to seven years in prison - the sentence to run consecutively with a 25-year term for his federal conviction on a California bank robbery.

Schreiber's personal and professional relationship with Montellano was apparently not the only connection which she had to gangs.

During his testimony at a murder trial in April, 1979, Art Beltran — reputed to be the third highest ranking member of the Nuestra Familia gang - said that Schreiber had asked him to lie on the witness stand in an earlier trial before she became a judge.[15] Beltran's comments about Schreiber came during a trial for another gang execution case. Beltran had been testifying for over an hour on his gang activities, his trials, his times in prison, and the chain of command of the Nuestra Familia when he made his startling remarks about Schreiber.[16]

That was not the last time Lenore Schreiber's name was mentioned in testimony by members of the gangs. In July of 1981, a hearing was held in another gang murder case. On trial were Alfredo Sosa, Manuel Torres, and Robert Salas — charged with the killing of Gilbert Roybal - all members of the Mexican Mafia (EME).[17] During the hearing, another member of the gang, Ramon Mendoza, testified that Schreiber had smuggled drugs to Sosa and Torres while they were in the Fresno County jail.[18] Phil Officer, the prosecutor in that case, was surprised by Mendoza's comments.[19] According to Mendoza the drugs involved included heroin and cocaine, and Schreiber had confirmed to him that they were delivered.[20] Mendoza also testified that Schreiber had carried a message back from Sosa. Mendoza said the message was that Sosa wanted Lupe Esqueda "hit". Esqueda was the common-law wife of the victim in the case, Gilbert Roybal, and had witnessed the crime. Her death would have eliminated the key witness in the case against the three gang members.[21]

In response to the accusations, Schreiber made a public statement that the charges were preposterous, that "Anyone who knows me knows my very strong sense of basically (being) against anything to do with violence, the death penalty..."[22] Schreiber also implied that the testimony had been planted by the District Attorney's office as part of a vendetta. They wanted to get her, she claimed, because she had humiliated members of that office during trials while she was a defense attorney. Her enemies, she said, also disliked her because of her Jewish heritage and because she had friends who were members of minorities.[23]

The feud over the Mendoza testimony became so heated that the D.A.'s office refused to conduct any felony hearings before her court, due to her "obvious animosity" toward the D.A.'s office.[24] Schreiber denied the District Attorney's peremptory challenges. The District Attorney's office then refused to prosecute any cases before her, and the cases were temporarily dropped. The matter was brought before Presiding Superior Court Judge Charles F. Hamlin in Fresno who ruled that Schreiber had exceeded her authority in insisting that she hear those cases.[25]

On January 21, 1982, Judge Lenore Schreiber announced that she would resign her judgeship rather than face the voters in a re-election campaign. She stated that she would return to private law practice, specializing in "feminist law."[26]

CHAPTER SEVEN

A FEW JUDICIOUS REMARKS

(To protect the privacy of the victims in the following case — privacy which has already been too often invaded — their names have been fictionalized.)

Being on the receiving end of obscene phone calls and sexual harassment can be a frightening experience. It is worse if that abuse comes from a powerful political figure with enough influence to get you fired from your job.

For over four and a half years, B M and her husband, D M suffered just such humiliation and fear.

They had come to California in 1972 from an impoverished life in Ohio. B M was able to find a low-paying job with the California State Legislature in 1972, but D remained unemployed. In 1973 Mrs. M was hired as a staff secretary by then Senator Robert Stevens. She won several promotions because of her competence as a secretary. In 1974, she became Senator Stevens' personal secretary.[1]

In August of 1974, Stevens helped arrange a job for D M as a Sergeant-at-Arms for the Legislature.[2] The Ms were grateful to the Senator, but they and the Senator understood that Stevens had tremendous power over their livelihood.

Influence over the Ms' career was only a very small part of Stevens' political clout. Robert Stevens was elected to the State Assembly in 1962 and re-elected in 1964. In 1966 he successfully ran for the State Senate, where he remained until 1976. Among the many positions of power which he had, at one time or another while a Senator, was that of Chairman of the Joint Legislative Ethics Committee.[3]

Stevens' political influence was based largely on his maverick liberal Republicanism. Frequently siding with the Democrats on critical issues, Stevens earned a large backlog of political IOUs. This became more pronounced when Jerry Brown was elected Governor. On major tax bills and farm labor issues, Stevens became the deciding vote for Jerry Brown's programs. Stevens also entered the Federal level political arena during the 1976 Republican Presidential nomination race. Stevens, a Republican legislator from Ronald Reagan's home state, wrote a letter for President Ford criticizing Reagan. Ford used the letter in the New Hampshire primary contest. Stevens also traveled on Ford's behalf, attacking Reagan in speeches in several states.[4]

Political observers at the time commented that Stevens appeared to be trying to line himself up for either a state or federal judgeship.

While his maneuvering never paid off in a federal bench appointment, Jerry Brown did repay his political debts to Stevens by appointing him as a judge of the Norwalk (Los Angeles) Superior Court on July 7, 1977.

B and D M learned what it means to tangle with such political power - and how hard it is for ordinary citizens to protect themselves from personal abuse by the powerful.

For the Ms, the problem started in January, 1975.[5] Mrs. M, at that time Stevens' personal secretary, was called to Stevens' office. He talked to her about some of his intimate personal problems.[6] She wasn't too concerned about that and other similar conversations at first. But the numerous talks gradually changed from revelation of his personal problems to explicit "sexual fantasies" and suggestions.[7]

Mrs. M complained to her fellow workers about the problem, and wrote a note to Stevens asking him to stop.[8] Stevens became very upset about the letter and told B M never to write about his sexual remarks again. But Stevens didn't stop making the remarks. He continued the lewd comments face-to-face with both D and B M and even began calling them at their home to make obscene suggestions.[9]

The California Commission on Judicial Performance, which investigated Stevens' conduct in an inquiry in the summer of 1980, described Stevens' harassment of the Ms. Stevens, the Commission stated, "Used vulgar and offensive language of an explicit sexual nature." He continually talked about "his own previous sexual experiences; his own sexual fantasies and desires; and his proposals that both of the (Ms) engage in sexual activity with him and other persons." Stevens "explicitly referred to the Ms' own sexual relationship and their private parts, as well as to his own and those of others; he made frequent and enthusiastic references to

45

oral sex, group sex, interracial sex, and homosexual sex." And, the Commission continued, Stevens' remarks were "principally in vulgar and offensive 'street' language."[10]

Stevens admitted that he had made the remarks, but called them "fantasizing. Sex fantasy, I suppose."[11] Stevens claimed that the Ms had not objected to the conversations, but the Commission on Judicial Performance inquiry found otherwise. The Commission report stated: B and D M "did not initiate any of these conversations; they did not welcome them, consent to them, or freely acquiesce in them, but repeatedly objected to (Stevens) and others about them. The (Ms) were harassed and annoyed by these conversations, and they suffered distress on account of them. Their distress was aggravated by the (Ms') fear of job retaliation for any complaint they might make against (Stevens)."[12]

It was in early 1976 that Stevens' comments to Mrs. M became more frequent and vulgarly suggestive. At first she mentioned it to the other members of the Senator's staff. Things had been so bad that Mrs. M would even ask members of the staff to stay in the office with her after 5 p.m. if Senator Stevens was still present. Her coworkers asked if she wanted them to do anything about the situation. Fearing for her job and that of her husband, Mrs. M said, no, and opted to wait out the short remainder of the Senator's term.[13]

Shortly before Stevens retired from the Senate the situation became too difficult for Mrs. M to bear. Her husband, D, confronted Stevens and told him to leave B alone. Stevens instead told D M to back down, reminding him that the jobs of both B and D could be affected.[14]

It was after this confrontation with Stevens that the Senator began making telephone calls to the Ms. Still they were afraid to make any more complaints, knowing that even their future jobs depended upon Steven's recommendation.[15]

During 1977 the Ms tried on their own to discourage Stevens from making his obscene phone calls. Even though Stevens was out of the Senate and became a judge later that year, he continued the calls on an almost weekly basis — although there were lapses of several months.[16] The Ms changed their phone number twice during that period, each time getting an unlisted number. But Stevens had access to state records which included those new phone numbers. They also tried not answering the phone at home.[17]

Finally, in April of 1979, the Ms had enough. They decided to start complaining until they found a way to stop the harassment. First they went to the office of Assembly Speaker Leo McCarthy. McCarthy suggested that the Ms tape the calls from Stevens for proof. They agreed to do so. The first taped conversation included comments by Stevens of his "sexual prowess" with high ranking state officials. To protect those people, the Ms destroyed that tape. In the meantime, however, McCarthy's office staff began checking into the credibility of the Ms. D M learned of this and became afraid to go back to McCarthy's office for more help. McCarthy's staff learned that M had a good record, but didn't pursue the matter since the Ms didn't return.

In 1978 D M mentioned the matter to members of the Assembly Rules Committee staff. That staff, believed the situation was in the past, and took no action. Next the Ms, who are Black, complained to the Black Legislative Caucus. With no help from that group, they decided to go to the State Police, and to the Governor's office.[19]

On August 24, 1979 D M went to the State Police Office in the capitol building. He was told to bring in the tapes he had made of the telephone conversations, but no police report was made. He immediately went to the Governor's office and met with Percy Pinkney, the Governor's assistant for community affairs. M was promised that the Governor's office would look into the matter.[20]

That same afternoon Stevens, by then a Brown appointed judge, made another call to B M, calling her at her job in the office of Assemblyman Gerald Felando. B M taped that conversation, and D immediately brought the tape to the State Police. J. Anthony Kline, then Brown's legal affairs secretary was told about the problem and the tapes. (Kline was later appointed by Brown to the San Francisco Superior Court in 1980 and elevated to Presiding Justice of the Court of Appeal in 1982.) He called the director and chief counsel for the Commission on Judicial Performance, Jack Frankel.[21]

Finally, it seemed the wheels were turning to correct the situation and stop the harassment. But that evening the Ms received a call from one of Brown's secretaries. They were told by her that, "We're returning your tapes. You have broken the law and could be subject to a $10,000 fine."[22] Brown's staff, when later questioned about this by reporters, claimed that it was just a "friendly warning." "We wanted them to be aware that there could be legal problems."[23] But the law specifically allows such tapes to be made, even without the knowledge of the caller, in order to obtain evidence of obscene phone calls. Those tapes are legally admissible as evidence in court.

The friendly warning from the Governor's Office wasn't the only one the Ms received. D M received two calls on August 30, 1979, from an unknown man with a southern accent who called himself "Sledge, as in hammer." In the first call, made to M at work, "Sledge" warned him that "I'm calling from within the building to show how close I can get to you. You can go to the fuzz, but back-off." D M immediately reported it to the State Police capitol building office. Shortly after making that report, D M received another call from "Sledge" who said, "I told you not to do that."[24]

The Ms ignored the warnings and pressed the matter with the Commission on Judicial Performance. The Commission filed a formal request for an investigation with the California Attorney General's Office. The Ms also filed a complaint with the Sacramento District Attorney.

Now the press learned of the scandal. They also learned that the Ms weren't the only ones harassed by Robert Stevens over the years. In an article in the *Los Angeles Herald Examiner* on October 22, 1979, reporters Linda Breakstone and Terry Pristin wrote that they had spoken with three women who had been subjected to obscene phone calls from Stevens, including comments about touching and grabbing parts of their bodies. Those women told the reporters and law enforcement investigators that Stevens had also threatened them with loss of their jobs. According to the *Los Angeles Herald Examiner* reporters, those three women also found no one would listen to their complaints.

Finally, a panel of three judges was appointed by the California Supreme Court to investigate the affair. The judges on the panel were Judge William Biddick, Jr. of the San Joaquin Superior Court; Judge William E. Byrne of the El Dorado County Superior Court; and retired Appellate Justice Preston Devine of San Francisco. The panel submitted its report to the Commission on Judicial Performance on August 7, 1980. Entitled "Inquiry Concerning Judge No. 43," their report found that the Ms were telling the truth about the incidents and that they had been harassed by obscene comments from Robert Stevens.

The Commission on Judicial Performance voted to recommend a censure of Stevens by the Supreme Court. Six members of the Commission voted for the censure, three for Stevens removal from the bench.[25] The Supreme Court issued a censure of Judge Stevens. Unfortunately, a censure does not remove a judge, nor does it subject him to a fine, loss of salary, or any other punishment.

Wikipedia reports that Judge Stevens "left the bench in 1981 after being censured for making unwanted obscene phone calls to employees of the California Legislature."

CHAPTER EIGHT

JUDICIAL INDISCRETION

Lewis Alston Wenzell seemed the philosophical and social archetype of Jerry Brown's preference for judicial appointments. Appointed to the San Diego Municipal Court in 1978 at the age of 35, Wenzell was "modernistic" in his judicial views and personal manners.

He had graduated from the Northwestern University Law School of Chicago in 1967 with a J.D., and an L.L.M. degree in 1969. He began practicing law in 1967 in Illinois. In 1972 he moved to San Diego and became a Senior Trial Attorney in the Federal Defender's Office. An expert defense lawyer, he joined the San Diego Criminal Defense Lawyers Club. In 1976 he wrote a chapter in the Public Defenders' Source Book.

Shortly after his appointment it became apparent that Wenzell was destined for quite a future in the Jerry Brown Judiciary. On February 2, 1979, just a year after taking the Municipal Bench he was selected by Jerry Brown's Supreme Court Chief Justice, Rose Bird, to serve a two-year term on the California Judicial Council — the administrative agency of the state's judiciary. Such an honor is usually reserved for veteran members of the courts. Of course, by then Wenzell did have more experience on the bench than did Rose Bird when she became Chief Justice. Wenzell also became a member of the Governing Committee of the Council for Judicial Education and Research.

But the liberal jurist's promising career was put in serious doubts by a scandal revealed in August of 1981. During a grand jury investigation of a prostitution ring in San Diego, it was discovered that the judge had been a regular customer of such services since at least 1977. The testimony heard by the grand jury luridly described repeated bizarre behavior by Wenzell. So bizarre that even decadent elements of society would question his legal, moral, and psychological fitness to be a judge.

Under oath, Vanessa Penny described her long-term relationship with Wenzell. The following pages are verbatim quotations from her testimony to the grand jury. Because of the extremely offensive nature of the acts described, you may wish to skip the next few pages. The authors sincerely apologize for the necessity of including material which we know will cause as much revulsion in you as it did us. These quotations are included here because it is otherwise impossible to convey the degree of immorality, perversion, and possible psychological problems involved. The questions were asked before the San Diego Grand Jury by Hugh E. Mc-Manus, Deputy District Attorney, San Diego County.

All the answers were given by Vanessa Penny.

Excerpts from the Testimony of Vanessa Penny
Before the San Diego Grand Jury
Tuesday, July 7, 1981

Q. Now, during this period of time, from 1976 until today, did you ever meet a person by the name of Lewis Wenzell?

A. Yes. I met him on an outcall when I was working for the Executive Suite Massage in 1977 ...

Q. Can you tell us what happened when you met Lewis Wenzell as best you can recall? ...

A. Okay. The first time he paid me for the massage, and then –

Q. Where did you go?

A. I went to his home ...

Q. And did he introduce himself to you and tell you who he was? ...

A. Well, at that time he was an attorney, and yes, he had -- he introduced himself as Lewis Wenzell.

Q. And when you gave a massage, was he nude?

A. Yes.

Q. Were you?

A. Yes ...

Q. How much did he pay you?

A. Well, the massage was $60 and for anything else it was $100.

Q. Was there anything else at that time?

A. Yes. We had oral sex, and then we would -- he asked me to masturbate his anus with my hand.

Q. And did you do that?

A. Yes ...

Q. Did you see him any time after that?

A. Several times ... I say within the years I have seen him anywhere from 20 to 25 times. ... (h)e never paid me under a hundred and the most he paid was $300.

Q. When he paid you the $300, was there anything special about that time?

A. Yes. It was something unusual that I have never done before. He asked me to -— he asked me to urinate in his mouth and he asked me to shit on his belly. ... He would take it and he would use it on his penis ... to make himself come.

Q. Was there anything else that he would have you do on all these other occasions as far as lubricating up your fist? ...

A. He wanted me to stick my whole hand in his anus, in his ass. ...

Q. Was that something that was done every time you went?

A. Yes. ...

Q. ... Have you ever been arrested?

A. Yes. ...

Q. And have you ever been in his (Wenzell's) court?

A. I went to his court, and then -- at first I didn't recognize him, and then -- ... I saw him up there and I said, wow, his face looked very familiar.

Q. Did Judge Wenzell, did he ever take any pictures of you?

A. Yes. ... I saw one and he just took it from my -- from my waist down, with my legs open. ...

Q. Would he sometimes, Judge Wenzell, would he sometimes pay you by check?

A. Sometimes, and then he would pay half cash ...

Q. Let me show you a series of checks that we have covering 1980. There is (sic) five of them from Exhibit 35.

The first one is check 1545 dated January 14, 1980, for $200 made out to Vanessa Penny. Is that one of the checks that Lewis Wenzell gave to you?

A. Yes it is. ... That was for the time when he asked me to -- to -- yeah. Do I have to say it?

Q. Well, at the time that you talked about before?

A. Right. ...

Q. Now, during the time that you were having sex for money with Judge Wenzell, did he ever -- were there ever any conversations between you and he about the fact that prostitution was illegal, that it was illegal to have sex for money?

A. No. ...

Q. Did you have any feelings based upon the fact that you knew he was a judge that you were not going to get in trouble for any prostitution that you did?

A. With him I didn't think I would get in trouble. ...

Q. When was the last time that you had contact with Judge Wenzell?

A. March of 1981 ... We just had the regular thing but he paid me in cash. ...

53

Q. Now, did there come a time when you talked with Judge Wenzell about the fact that you worked for Betty Ballard, Lottie Ballard?

A. Yes, I have discussed with him that I was working for Cameo Models at one time. ...

Q. And can you tell us what the nature of that conversation was? What happened? What did he say and what did you say?

A. Well, I was talking about how "B.B." was going to get busted for pimping and pandering because of the way she paid the girls for the calls, and there was just a plain conversation with him about that, about Cameo Models. ...

Q. When was it that you worked for Cameo, as best you can recall?

A. I think it was in 1979.

Q. So he knew in 1979 that you were working for Cameo because you told him?

A. Uh huh.

Q. Now, during your conversations over the years with Judge Wenzell, were there ever any conversations about the danger of working in prostitution or working for outcall agencies?

A. Well, one time I went over there and he told me to be very careful because he had heard that our parlor was going to be raided or the red light abatement. They was going to come through and a lot of girls was going to get busted and go to jail. He told me to be very careful because he heard that something to that effect was going to happen. ...

Q. And some time after that were there a lot of parlors closed --

A. Oh, yes. Oh, yes.

Q. - from the red light abatement?

A. Uh huh.

Q. And was one of them the one you were working for?

A. No. They didn't even come to us. They didn't even come to us at all.

Q. But they came to almost everyone else in town?

A. Uh huh.

Q. Closed them down?

A. Uh huh.

The San Diego District Attorney's Office filed, on August 5, 1981, eight misdemeanor charges against Wenzell for solicitation of prostitution.

The District Attorney's Office did not file any charges of official corruption, but did mention in an official press release that "We found that the judge dismissed or acquitted on charges in almost all sex cases which came before him."

One of the sex related cases which Wenzell had heard and dismissed involved Lottie Ballard. Ballard was the owner of Cameo Models, for whom Vanessa Penny worked. Ballard was charged with two felony counts of prostitution in 1980. Vanessa Penny had testified that, while engaged in acts of prostitution with Judge Wenzell in 1979, she had told him that she worked through Ballard's agency. When the case against Ballard was brought before his court in 1980, Wenzell dismissed the charges, ruling that the police had entered her premises illegally.

Now, with charges of soliciting prostitution filed against him, Wenzell pled not guilty and adamantly refused to resign his judgeship. Instead, Wenzell, through his attorney Peter Hughes, complained that the District Attorney's Office was prosecuting the case "as harshly and embarrassingly as possible" as a means of destroying his effectiveness as a judge. Hughes filed a motion with the court hearing Wenzell's case to have the District Attorney's Office removed from prosecuting Wenzell.

Wenzell's stubborn refusal to step down, even temporarily, from the bench proved an embarrassment to his fellow San Diego judges. Two days after the charges against Wenzell were filed, those judges voted not to assign any cases to Wenzell. In the face of that decision, Wenzell insisted on continuing to hear cases. On September 25, 1981 his fellow judges were forced to reverse themselves — as there was no legal provision allowing them to prevent Wenzell from continuing to perform as a judge.

Presiding San Diego Municipal Court Judge Kenneth Jones stated that he was required to assign cases to Wenzell because "there's no precedent and no code section authorizing" non-assignment. Others in the legal community (other judges and lawyers) had expressed "concern that the court was doing something illegal (by not assigning cases to Wenzell) and the judges finally decided our job is not to determine what's moral. It's our job to determine what's legal."

In early October, Wenzell's trial began in Newport Beach, Orange County — where it had been transferred to assure Wenzell a fair trial away from the publicity his situation had received in San Diego.

During the trial additional testimony showed that Wenzell's acts with Vanessa Penny were not unusual for him. Three other women, Guadelupe Palmer, Marily Wyand, and Nancie Mazzei testified that they had performed a variety of acts — including some they were reluctant to describe - with Wenzell. Palmer testified that her relationship with Wenzell was so frequent and of such long standing that she considered Wenzell to be "like a boyfriend" instead of a customer.

On October 10, 1981, Judge Lewis Alston Wenzell was found guilty by the Newport Beach jury of five misdemeanor counts of soliciting prostitution.

Immediately after the verdict was announced, Wenzell's attorney said that the case would be appealed — and that Wenzell would continue to sit on the San Diego Municipal Court bench during the appeal. Wenzell's fellow judges on the San Diego court unanimously, and publicly, called on him to resign. They were joined by the law enforcement officials in San Diego. Still Wenzell refused to step down. He did agree to take a short, paid leave of absence — but resumed his role as judge on October 22, 1981, only 12 days after his conviction.

The Wenzell matter was brought before the California Commission on Judicial Performance - the body which reviews complaints against judges and recommends disciplinary action against judges to the State Supreme Court. On December 3, 1981 the Commission adopted a resolution recommending that the Supreme Court suspend Wenzell from office, and that he be removed from office after the conviction became final. But there's the rub. On appeal Lewis Wenzell became the beneficiary of the liberal judicial rules which the courts had adopted over the years. His conviction was overturned by the Appellate Division of the Orange County Superior Court on June 23, 1982.

Judge Wenzell continued to be a sitting member of the California Judiciary. His removal now could only be accomplished by impeachment and conviction by the California Legislature, or by recall and defeat at the polls by the voters — both extremely difficult and rare occurrences.

In the meantime legal rulings continued to be made by

a judge who at the least had shown utter disrespect for the courts, the law, morality, and decency — as well as showing a lack of respect for himself and the women with whom he dealt. We must also be concerned that the judge either suffered from a psychological problem — with all that implies for his judgment — or subscribes to a libertine code of non-ethics which must affect his decisions. Whether or not Jerry Brown could have known about Wenzell's sexual penchants, Brown surely was aware of Wenzell's legal philosophy — those views were a major reason Brown appointed Wenzell to the bench, and why Rose Bird quickly aided his career.

Fortunately, the people of San Diego wouldn't stand for a man of Wenzell's caliber sitting in judgment of legal issues. Led by a private attorney, Henry Cunningham, Deputy District Attorney Charles Patrick, and the San Diego Tribune, a recall drive gathered an estimated 54,000 signatures to successfully place a recall of Wenzell on the November 1982 General Election Ballot.

Even after the recall qualified, Wenzell at first was determined to fight to keep his seat on the bench. After an experience of soul-searching, however, Wenzell changed his mind and resigned. Explaining that decision Wenzell said "...I resolved to fight this attempt to unseat me because I was confident the voters could be relied upon to recognize the hypocrisy with which misdemeanor charges against me and other attendant matters were pursued and exploited and to express their criticism by retaining me in office...I have now, however, decided that I must forego the luxury of vindication by the people of San Diego."

CHAPTER NINE

TWO WHITES DON'T MAKE IT RIGHT

Trouble often comes in pairs, as police officers and battered children learned in early 1982. Within days of each other two judges, who were also former law partners, issued separate controversial rulings. One released a convicted cop-killer. The other minimized the seriousness of death caused by child-abuse.

On May 23, 1973 Oakland Police Officer Robert Blan was killed in the line of duty. Robert Earl Simmons was arrested for the crime. In December of 1973 he was convicted of second degree murder. Simmons' defense lawyer was Clinton W. White, who later was appointed by Governor Jerry Brown as Presiding Justice of the San Francisco Court of Appeals. Clinton White had a partner in his law firm, James S. White.[1] James White was also appointed to the bench by Jerry Brown — as a judge for the Oakland-Piedmont Municipal Court in 1979.

Simmons, the convicted cop-killer, served six and one-half years in the state prison. He was released and placed on parole in February of 1980.[2]

Two years later, on January 26, 1982, Robert Simmons was pulled over for speeding. He allegedly drew a gun on the two officers who had stopped him. The officers arrested Simmons for assault with a deadly weapon against a police officer and possession of a loaded firearm. Because Simmons was a felon it was illegal for him to possess any gun. Upon arresting Simmons, the officers searched his car and found a second gun.[3]

Common sense would assume that a convicted murderer of a police officer, who is arrested for threatening two other officers with a gun, would be treated sternly by any judge.

The Alameda County District Attorney's Office sought a bail of $19,000 against Simmons. Instead Judge James White, the former partner of Simmons' 1973 defense lawyer, decided to release Simmons on his own recognizance — free without bail. Three days later Simmons was again picked up by the police — this time with another person who happened to have a gun in his possession.[4]

Members of the Oakland Police Force were outraged. On Thursday, February 4, 1982, over a hundred off-duty officers and other citizens gathered in front of the court house for a silent protest against Judge James White's actions. One of the organizers of the protest, Sgt. Lou Clark, summed up the views of the crowd. Police, he said, "are tired of being victims out there, and we're tired of decent citizens being victimized by the same violent people over and over."[5]

Judge James White reacted with a tirade from his judicial bench against the silent demonstration. "They have fed the fires of bigotry and racial hatred which exist throughout this community," he said, "This dastardly and despicable conduct (note: He was referring to the peaceful protest) has been engaged in for their own political purposes.[6]

"We've witnessed a small group of people rekindle the emotions of hate, anger, and grief," the judge continued, "and renew the heartaches and feelings of deep loss in the hearts and minds of the dead officer's family."[7]

One of the protesters, however, was Nancy Blan, the widow of the officer killed by Simmons in 1973. Mrs. Blan was pleased by the turnout and the concern shown by the crowd. "The numbers here," she said, "show the anger we all feel regarding the release of a cop-killer."[8]

While the judge called the protestors despicable, dastardly bigots, he had kinder words for convicted cop-killer Simmons. The protest, Judge James White said, was aimed at discrediting the judiciary, "and me particularly, simply because I have performed my judicial function in a fair and just manner in considering and granting this poor unfortunate man his release. He is poor because he has no money, and poor because he has no spirit."[9]

The judge's compassion was truly heartwarming ... to Robert Simmons anyway, if not to Nancy Blan.

Possibly Judge White believed Simmons, who had killed one policeman and was charged with pulling a gun on two others, when Simmons said, "I'm not a desperado who goes around shooting policemen. I have nothing against police."[10]

Prosecutor Rock Harmon pointed out an irony in the case. If Simmons were convicted of the two gun possession and assault charges, he could be sentenced to ten years and eight months in prison, longer than he got for killing Officer Blan in 1973.[11]

David R. McGill, who served with Officer Blan on the Oakland Police force, wrote the following letter to the *Oakland Tribune* which was published on March 5, 1982. It needs no further comment.

"Ever since Judge White first made his decision to release Robert Simmons on his own recognizance, I have remained silent. Any expression on my part seemed shallow in comparison to the disgust, anger, and shame I feel.

"I am the police officer who covered Officer Blan the night of his murder. I was present when Robert Simmons attempted to run down another police officer with his car, while trying to escape. At that point I was in a position to kill Simmons, but I held my fire. After Simmons was apprehended, he would not give me the location where he had left Blan to die. It took considerable time to find Blan and get medical attention. He was found shot three times.

"Judge White has been quoted as stating that he didn't know the facts of the murder but, 'The officer killed must have started the fight.' With the same lack of knowledge, he said, 'The jury probably didn't have the guts to go for a manslaughter charge because the victim was a police officer.'

"The comments of Judge White spout the bigotry, racism and hatred that he accused the Oakland Police Department of practicing. He seems to be using his position to fight against law enforcement.

"On his own, White is not significant enough for me to take issue with, but Governor Jerry Brown has appointed several others like him. The appointment of ignorant judges like White only contributes to lawlessness.

"I knew Bob Blan well. I worked with him from his appointment until his death. I watched him treat all citizens decently, including the lowest elements of society.

"Bob Blan put Simmons in the back seat of his car, which had no cage. Out of consideration, he did not handcuff Simmons. Bob didn't feel there were people in the world who would kill him over a $90 traffic warrant, or for just being a police officer.

"Unlike Judge White, I know Simmons and I knew Blan. I speak with knowledge and from facts. White clearly shows his prejudices and he, and individuals like him, should not be placed in positions where their ignorance and bigotry can be allowed to affect the lives of decent citizens regardless of race.

David R. McGill
Oakland"

It may be puzzling how a judge could be appointed who is described by attorneys who have practiced before him as, at best, an average judge who has not displayed a high caliber legal intellect.[12]

Judge James White had, however, had been a long-time friend and strong political supporter of Oakland Mayor Lionel Wilson. He had also been a long-time associate and former law partner of Justice Clinton White. Those connections, it seems, were enough to win James White an appointment by Governor Brown.[13]

Having the support of Justice Clinton W. White, however, might not seem a great asset, judging from Clinton White's record. In an eye opening coincidence of timing, Appeals Court Justice Clinton W. White — the senior partner of the former law firm with James White — issued a controversial ruling which set a precedent favoring defendants accused of child abuse.

In late January of 1982 Justice White wrote the opinion for the San Francisco Court of Appeals stating that child beating and abuse are not inherently dangerous and life-threatening, and therefore can't be used as a basis for a second degree murder conviction.[14]

Three-year old Kareemah Joseph died on February 11, 1979 of beatings which a court found were delivered by her father, Harold Joseph.

Harold Joseph had attempted to convince the police and medical investigators that Kareemah had slipped twice during a bath, each time hitting her head. That, he claimed, caused her death. However, hospital pathologists discovered Kareemah had numerous bruises besides the two head injuries. She also had a lacerated liver and suffered retinal hemorrhaging caused by an injury.[15]

The case against Harold Johnson was based on the findings of the pathologists, the testimony of Johnson's wife that he had also beaten their son, and expert testimony on child abuse.

To obtain a second-degree murder conviction the prosecution must show that the murder was done with malice — evil intent. If a person repeatedly attacks and injures an adult, and eventually one of those attacks results in death, malice is provable.

The expert testimony in the Johnson case was to show that little Kareemah had been subjected to the "battered child syndrome."

As explained by Deputy District Attorney Robert Platt, the prosecutor in the Johnson Trial, child abuse cases are largely circumstantial and expert testimony is crucial. "The battered child syndrome," Platt explained, "provides a medical situation in which doctors can look at the records and say, 'This was not an accident.' It doesn't identify the perpetrator, it only establishes that a criminal act has taken place."[16]

That expert testimony shows if a crime fits the pattern of child abuse. A history of child abuse and the unlikelihood of two serious head injuries occurring during a bath are important elements to prove the death was not accidental and was due to malice.

The court led by Justice White, however, decided that such testimony should not be admitted in cases involving death from child abuse. "The doctor's opinion amounted to impermissible expert testimony on whether the (defendant) was telling the truth," White wrote in his opinion.[17]

Deputy District Attorney Platt complained that "What the court is telling me here is that I can't put the testimony into evidence because the doctor has called the defendant a liar, and I can't prove my case that way."[18]

Justice White ordered a new trial for Johnson, but with the requirements that it be for manslaughter, not murder, and that the expert testimony not be presented.

Perhaps we should feel comforted that our rights are protected so unflinchingly in the courts of Judge James White and his former partner, Justice Clinton White. Unfortunately, we'll never hear the other side of the story from Officer Blan and little Kareemah Johnson.

CHAPTER TEN

"THE JUDGE CRIMINALS LOVE"

Henry Ramsey was born on January 22, 1934, in Florence, South Carolina. Abandoned by his natural parents at the age of three months, Ramsey was raised by poor but hard working foster parents. Much of his youth was spent in Rocky Mountain, North Carolina, until he dropped out of school after the ninth grade. After leaving school, he joined the Air Force, serving from 1951 to 1955. It was the Air Force which brought him to California. Those were bad years for Ramsey. He describes himself in those years as a "junior thug" and says that he "drank a lot and fought a lot."[1]

The next ten years were better for Henry. He went back to school and got his high school diploma. He also earned a BA in Philosophy, and his LLB from Boalt Hall School of Law of the University of California in 1963.[2]

Following law school, Ramsey moved through a succession of jobs as an attorney, and in 1973 he was elected to the Berkeley City Council. He was also a member of the Board of Directors of the American Civil Liberties Union of Northern California from 1971 to 1973.[3]

In short, Henry Ramsey was the kind of person Jerry Brown wanted to name to the California judiciary — with an underprivileged background, and certifiably liberal.

The only black mark on his record was a conviction for "disturbing the peace." That incident involved a verbal altercation with his ex-wife at 10:00 p.m. one night. Ramsey was upset that Evelyn Jones (Ramsey) had brought their children back at such a late hour. After a loud conversation, he ended the argument by firing three shots into Evelyn's car (which was unoccupied at the time). His shots blew out the two right tires of Evelyn's 1964 Rambler. The police report quoted Ramsey as saying to Evelyn "I'm going to kill you." Of course, he didn't.[4]

Ramsey subsequently paid a $100 fine in Municipal Court, and the Richmond Police Department records were marked: "Cleared by Arrest."[5]

Some months later, the police were again called to Ramsey's house where he charged that Evelyn Jones had yelled at him and his girlfriend, a Miss Mason, and threatened to beat up Miss Mason. Evelyn's story was different. She admitted yelling, but says that Miss Mason kicked her in the stomach.[6]

The Richmond Police Department officers who were dispatched to the scene, T. Walters and R. Parrich, reported that the argument was over "payment of child support." They also did not feel that Ramsey's charges against his ex-wife were worth bothering with and "suggest(ed that) this report be filed." Their report was approved by their superior and filed as "inactive."[7]

On September 18, 1980, Governor Jerry Brown appointed Henry Ramsey to the Alameda County Superior Court. In 1982 he filed for re-election to that position, and was challenged by Alameda County Assistant District Attorney Albert (Bud) Meloling. Meloling was a top-notch prosecutor who had been picked twice by the California District Attorney's Association as "Prosecutor of the Year". Meloling had tried more than 300 felony cases, including 61 murder cases.

Meloling did not attack Ramsey on his misdemeanor conviction but rather focused on Ramsey's liberal sentencing policies.[8]

One case questioned by Meloling was that of Jimmy Springer in 1981. Springer was convicted by a jury of second-degree murder. Ramsey reduced that conviction to manslaughter. That decision created a barrage of criticism from prosecutor Jerry Curtis, the victim's family, and a juror — Andrea Randall — who wrote to the court urging that the second-degree murder conviction stand.[9]

Ramsey said that he reduced the conviction because the defendant was "highly jealous" and may have killed his girlfriend "in a rage." That despite evidence presented by the prosecution that Springer had told his cousin that he planned to kill his girlfriend, Ms. Davis. Prosecutor Curtis also showed that Springer had broken Ms. Davis' arm while beating her the year before, and that he had choked her and threatened to kill her shortly before the stabbing.[10]

The jury reached its decision even though Ramsey had

prevented the jury from hearing evidence that Springer had often severely beaten Ms. Davis. Ramsey did, however, allow the jury to hear of Springer's various threats on her life.[11]

Another case attacked by Meloling involved a Liberian national who was convicted by a jury of sodomizing a retarded 16-year-old boy. Ramsey sentenced the man to nine months in the county jail. However, Ramsey then took the highly unusual step of granting the defendant's motion to prevent the sodomy conviction from being used against the criminal in a deportation hearing.[12]

Ramsey granted the motion even though the prosecutor pointed out that: (1) the defendant was in the United States on a student visa, but had not been attending school for a year; (2) that the defendant had petty theft convictions in both Alameda and San Francisco Counties; (3) that the defendant had a pending petty theft charge in Hayward; and (4) at the time of the sodomy conviction, he was still on probation from a prior offense.

None of those facts swayed Ramsey, "the judge criminals love," as Meloling referred to him.[13]

But the facts about Ramsey's record were not strong enough to beat the political machine which supported Ramsey. Assembly Speaker Willie Brown, a Democrat, provided Ramsey with campaign support. So did a host of other local Democrats including Nicholas Petris and Oakland Mayor Lionel Wilson. Ramsey was also supported by 17 of the 30 Superior Court Judges, more than 13 local municipal court judges, and State Supreme Court Justices Cruz Reynoso, Frank Newman, and Allen Broussard (all three Brown appointees like Ramsey).[14]

On June 8, 1982 Superior Court Judge Henry Ramsey was re-elected by the people of Alameda County.

And we are left to ponder a quote from Judge Ramsey who said he used to dream of the day "we could get judges and jurors to apply the law as it is written." Bud Meloling couldn't have said it better.

Judge Ramsey went on to serve on the important Judicial Council of the State of California from 1988 to 1991 before he retired in 1999.

CHAPTER ELEVEN

YOUR PARENTS ARE SO PROUD OF YOU

Governor Jerry Brown attended a private fund raising party at the Northridge home of Milton and Beatrice Luros on June 28, 1981.[1] Two things set that function apart from most of the small political functions which a governor attends on a regular basis.

First, besides being a money raiser for Brown, the party was also a celebration that the Governor had just appointed Milton and Beatrice Luros's son, Michael Luros, to a new Municipal Court judgeship in Los Angeles less than three months earlier. Second, the party gained notoriety five days later from a *Daily News* headline: "One-time Porn Distributor Hosts Gov. Brown Fundraiser."[2]

Milton Luros had an extensive record of arrests on pornography and obscenity charges from 1959 on. He had been able to beat most of those charges in court or on appeal. But in 1977 his streak of legal luck ran out. He pleaded guilty to one count of aiding and abetting the sending of obscene material through the mail, for which he was fined $5,000 and given three years probation.[3]

All in all, Milton Luros still did well for himself. A Federal Grand Jury had indicted him on 31 counts of conspiracy to send obscene material through the mail and aiding and abetting the sending of such material.[4]

"His corporations together were the largest in the country as far as the production and distribution of sexually explicit materials," the *Daily News* quoted Sgt. Joseph F. Ganley, former head of the Los Angeles Police Department's Administrative Vice Unit.[5]

Ganley continued, "He is the past owner of a number of companies involved in the publishing and distribution of sexually explicit magazines. A lot of people who are major successful pornographers now worked for and learned the business from Luros."[6]

The Luros operation was so large that it also caught the attention of the Federal Bureau of Investigation. A retired Bureau agent confirmed that Luros operated one of - if not the - largest pornography operations in the entire country.

Luros's various California companies included London Press, Parliament News, Oxford Bindery, Academy Press, American Art Enterprises, the E.W.A.P., Inc. — which operates the Le Sex Shoppe book stores.[7] He was also reported to own a string of adult book stores in the Phoenix, Arizona area.[8]

In 1974 Parliament News had been a financial contributor to the Personal Freedom Political Fund, which is sometimes described as the porno dealers' political action committee. The Personal Freedom Political Fund had supported various political candidates who had been key supporters of legislation of interest to pornographers.[9]

At the time of the Brown fund raiser, the *Daily News* reported, a 1978 Red Light Abatement case was pending against the Le Sex Shoppe on Van Nuys Boulevard in Sherman Oaks. Milton and Beatrice Luros were identified as the building's owners and lessors. The *Daily News* further said that a July 1979 injunction was still in effect which prohibited the Le Sex Shoppe "from being operated for the purpose of the lewdness and from permitting either directly or indirectly any acts of lewdness." The injunction had been issued by Los Angeles Superior Court Judge George M. Dell.[10]

While Judge Dell did not attend the Brown/Luros party, one judge who did attend said that at least three municipal court judges were in attendance. Of those only Municipal Court Judge Richard C. Hubbell spoke to the *Daily News* on the record. Hubbell acknowledged having heard rumors about the Luros's activities, but said that he attended because Michael Luros had asked him to and that "He (Brown) made an excellent appointment in Mike, I would anticipate he would be on the appellate bench."[11]

Mike Luros, however, was less outspoken. When reporters tried to talk to him, he simply stated "Really, as a matter of course I don't give interviews ... I really don't give interviews." — and then hung up.[12]

Mike Luros was described as "the most non-political person you could ever meet" by Hal Dash, Senior Vice President of Cerrell Associates — and a spokesman for Luros's campaign for re-election to the bench. (It seems that Mike was already expecting a tough fight in the election a year away.) What Mr. Dash failed to mention was that Mike Luros had already given Jerry Brown a $466.33 in-kind campaign contribution.[13]

The Brown camp was even more secretive. The people running his then-unofficial 1982 senatorial campaign refused to either confirm or deny that the Governor had attended the fund raiser — or even that one was held at the Luros's home.[14]

Gray Davis, Brown's Chief of Staff, did confirm that the campaign committee looks into the background of people who offer to hold fund-raisers. Davis said: "It is not our function to pass judgement on people, but we are mindful certain peoples' offers to help could become political liabilities and for that reason we reject their offers of assistance, not necessarily because we agree they are in any way bad people, but it's just not worth the additional political burden of defending someone's past activities." In short, Brown's Chief of Staff said that they would take anyone's money as long as they could get away with it politically. Bill Packer of the *Daily News*' Capitol Bureau put it this way: "Governor Edmund G. Brown, Jr. prefers to raise funds for his presidential and statewide campaigns behind closed doors and away from the 'piranhas' of the press, his top aide says."[15]

The Brown campaign proved the point when shortly after the article ran in the *Daily News*, Brown returned a $2,000 contribution to Milton Luros and a $1,800 contribution to Beatrice Luros because "The Governor was concerned about an appearance problem ..."[16]

But what of the appearance problem of the Governor of California appointing the son of a nationally prominent porno dealer to the bench?

Judge Hubbell said "whatever his father is or isn't shouldn't bear on his right to live his own life." These same sentiments were echoed by Chief of Staff Davis and by Byron Georgiou, Brown's legal affairs secretary. Besides, Mike Luros has never had anything to do with his dad and mom's business ... or has he?[17]

Milt Luros's attorney is David M. Brown of Fleishman, McDaniel, Brown and Weston. That firm has had a leading role in defending pornography cases under the banner of the First Amendment - Freedom of Speech. The firm was also a contributor to the Personal Freedom Political Fund — mentioned earlier.[18]

California Bar Association records show that Mike Luros used that law firm's address when he took the bar exams, and that Mike's license to practice law was issued to him at that address.[19]

We are justified in asking just what values and judgement did Mike's parents impart to him? And does the attendance by sitting judges at a political fund raiser at the home of a convicted porno king bring disrepute on the judiciary — a violation of the Cannons of Judicial Conduct.

Maybe Mike Luros should just have saved himself, the other judges, his parents, and the Governor a lot of undesirable publicity by staying out of politics, and not inviting anyone anywhere.

CHAPTER TWELVE

DEMOCRACY IN ACTION

The essence of democracy — at least by most people's understanding — is that government is the servant of the citizens and responds to their demands. We make our wishes known at the ballot box. When matters become particularly unsatisfactory, but too complex to place the blame accurately, the voters often react in the only logical and effective way — they "throw the rascals out." The revolt at the ballot box serves to bring in a new team, and to warn all government officials that they had better change their ways.

But some politicians have a way of sending an arrogant message back to the voters that they really don't give a damn what the people think.

During Brown's years as governor, the rise in crime, the tendency of many judges to grant wide protection of criminals' rights with little regard for the victims, and perceived politicization of the judiciary convinced many voters that certain judges should be kicked off the bench. In California, the voters eventually have the opportunity to remove judges through the ballot box. And with increasing frequency, the voters did just that.

While some of the judges defeated by the voters may have been unfairly caught up in an anti-judiciary, anti-crime atmosphere, a basic respect for democratic principles would seem to demand that the voters' wishes be followed.

Apparently, Governor Jerry Brown didn't agree.

In the June 4, 1978 election the voters removed seventeen judges from the California bench. Eight of those had been appointed by Governor Jerry Brown — who had himself been in office only three and one-half years. Those judges served out the remainder of their terms, leaving the bench in January, 1979. Nine months later, by September of that same year, four of those judges had been reappointed to other courts by Jerry Brown.[1]

By March of 1982, Brown had circumvented the decisions of the voters by re-appointing at least eight defeated judges: Fred Lucero and Stephen Manley of San Jose; Leonard Goldstein and Richard Hamilton of Orange County; Bruce Thompson of Ventura County; Armando Rodriguez of Fresno County; and Elva Soper and David Perez of Los Angeles.[2]

For obvious reasons, the Governor's office has not kept records (at least not publicly) of defeated judges who are reappointed.[3]

In fact, Jerry Brown has gone to some lengths to keep his re-nominees' previous defeats quiet. When Brown re-appointed Lucero and Hamilton, the announcement from his office mentioned that they had once been superior court judges but did not mention that they had been voted out of their judgeships. When Thompson and Goldstein were re-appointed, the Governor's office was careful not to mention that they had ever held their previous positions as superior court judges.[4]

In defense of his anti-democratic practice, Jerry Brown argued that "I have only done it when the people in the community, the legal community leaders, and the local newspapers, have come to me and endorsed the person as a good judge."[5] In other words, when the special interests of the lawyers and their allies in the press wanted a judge in office, Jerry Brown would follow their wishes, instead of the will of the people.

After all, Brown explained, the voters are ignorant. The voters defeated good judges because of "...usually some phony issue," Jerry says, "Some of them were defeated because they had Hispanic surnames. Goldstein lost because of some residency issue. You know, some voter in L.A. with a list of 20 judges to vote on isn't likely to study who's good and who isn't, or all the ins and outs of it."[6]

What should be remembered, however, is that the defeat of a sitting judge is still a rarity. The voters have proven quite selective in who they remove from the bench. Some were probably defeated because they were believed to be liberal judges appointed by a soft-on-crime governor. Others possibly because of a "phony" residency issue. Others, like Judge David Perez may have been removed because the people believed that they were not entirely fit for the office. Perez, his opponent in the election argued, had been involved in the shredding of police documents concerning citizen complaints against Los Angeles Police Department officers — that activity occurring while Perez served as a Deputy City Attorney before being named to the judiciary.[7]

Regardless of the reason for the defeat of the judges, the fact remains that the people very selectively removed them. The political elite may believe that they know better than the voters - but such an attitude must be recognized as subversive to the concept of democratic government.

But Jerry Brown's and his allies' undemocratic attitudes aren't limited to simply restoring their favored defeated jurists. Upset over the loss of Judge Perez, Jerry Brown and friends enacted a law to reduce criticism of judges. Prior to that law, opponents of judges could state their objections to the qualifications, decisions, and other actions of the sitting judges in a ballot statement sent out by the various county election departments to the voters. Governor Brown signed into law a bill forbidding any criticism of judicial opponents in the ballot statement.[8] That law would have protected the judiciary from scrutiny by what Brown regarded as ignorant voters — and would keep those voters uninformed and unable to make a careful decision about which judges to defeat and which to re-elect. Fortunately, the law was ruled unconstitutional by the courts themselves.

Jerry's attempt to gag critics of his judges was doubtlessly an expression of his faith in the democratic process.

BACKGROUND OF SOME JUDGES RE-APPOINTED BY JERRY BROWN[9]

GOLDSTEIN, LEONARD
Appointed: January 11, 1977 to Orange County Superior
  Court by Governor Jerry Brown
Defeated by Voters: June 6, 1978
Left Office: January 7, 1979
Re-appointed: January 8, 1979 to the North Orange County
  Municipal Court by Governor Jerry Brown

HAMILTON, RICHARD D.
Appointed: April 22, 1977 to Orange County Superior Court

by Governor Jerry Brown
Defeated by Voters: June 6, 1978
Left Office: January 7, 1979
Re-appointed: January 8, 1979 to the Orange County
Municipal Court by Governor Jerry Brown

LUCERO, FRED S.
Appointed: November 28, 1976 to the Santa Clara Count
Superior Court by Governor Jerry Brown
Defeated by Voters: June 6, 1978
Left Office: January 7, 1979
Re-appointed: April 5, 1979 to Santa Clara Municipal Court
by Governor Jerry Brown

MANLEY, STEPHEN V.
Appointed: June 1, 1977 to San Jose—Milpitas Municipal
Court by Governor Jerry Brown
Defeated by Voters: June 6, 1978
Left Office: January 7, 1979
Re-appointed: May 14, 1981 to San Jose Municipal Court
by Governor Jerry Brown

PEREZ, DAVID
Appointed: December 11, 1975 to the West Los Angeles
Municipal Court by Governor Jerry Brown
Defeated by Voters: June 3, 1980
Re-appointed: May 14, 1981 to the East Los Angeles
Municipal Court by Governor Jerry Brown

RODRIGUEZ, ARMANDO O.
Appointed: April 5, 1979 to the Fresno County Superior
Court by Governor Jerry Brown
Defeated by Voters: June 3, 1980
Left Office: December 29, 1980
Re-appointed: December 19, 1980 to the Fresno Municipal
Court by Governor Jerry Brown

SOPER, ELVA (AGUILAR)
Appointed: April 14, 1976 to the Palo Alto Municipal Court by
Governor Jerry Brown
Defeated by Voters: June 3, 1980
Left Office: January 4, 1981
Re-appointed: February 10, 1982 to the Los Angeles

Municipal Court by Governor Jerry Brown

THOMPSON, BRUCE A.
Appointed: February 2, 1978 to the Ventura County Superior
  Court by Governor Jerry Brown
Defeated by Voters: November 7, 1978
Left Office: January 7, 1979
Re-appointed: January 8, 1979 to the Ventura County
  Municipal Court by Governor Jerry Brown

CHAPTER THIRTEEN

JUDGES, POLITICS AND MONEY

In 1978, the *Los Angeles Times* reported the California Supreme Court was holding up politically sensitive cases until after the General Election in November. The alleged reason — Chief Justice Rose Bird was standing for re-election to her position and was running behind in the polls.

Following the election, Bird herself called on the Commission on Judicial Performance to conduct public hearings on the charges. The Commission exists to police the judiciary, to hear complaints about judges, and to recommend to the state Supreme Court the appropriate punishment. The Supreme Court may or may not follow the recommendations, as it chooses.

Because of the unprecedented review of the Supreme Court itself, rules for the investigation had to be hastily jerry-rigged by the California Judicial Council — which oversees the Commission on Judicial Performance.

In order for the Commission to adopt a recommendation or report, five affirmative votes must be cast from among the nine members. Prior to the investigation, Justice Racanelli, a member of the Commission, disqualified himself from the case. He was followed by Commission members Gehrels and Chodos. On the day of the Commission's final meeting during the investigation a fourth member, Judge Jerry Pacht was absent. That meant that it would take only one of the five remaining members to prevent a report of disciplinary recommendation against the Supreme Court.

One of the five remaining members was a Jerry Brown appointed "public member" — a non-judge — named Thomas Willoughby. Willoughby had supported Rose Bird during her confirmation hearings when she had just been appointed to the Chief Justice position. In that testimony Willoughby described Bird as a "valued friend." During her campaign in November of 1978 to remain on the Court, Willoughby had contributed to her cause.[1] It is not unlikely that Bird had encouraged Jerry Brown to arrange Willoughby's appointment to the Commission in the first place.

The Commission took no clear action. But several interesting facts did become public knowledge due to the hearings.

Justice Mathew Tobriner testified under oath that he "was never her (Rose Bird's) political advisor, nor did I participate one iota in her campaign." But it was learned that his wife had given $1,000 to Californians for the Court — a political committee supporting Rose Bird and the three other judges on the ballot in the November 1978 election.[2] Also during the election, Justice Tobriner himself had contacted the editor of the *San Francisco Examiner* to complain about an article critical of Bird. Tobriner had also helped to arrange meetings between Bird and the editorial board of major newspapers just prior to the election.

Supreme Court Justice Stanley Mosk, according to testimony of fellow Justice William Clark, had said in January of 1979 that "I told Matt (Tobriner) that it was obvious that cases were being held for filing after (the) election, and I told him it was obvious and if it were revealed he would pay the consequences." Unfortunately, we never heard Mosk's side of the story. Mosk filed suit to close the hearings of the Commission from the public. He succeeded in his suit, after numerous appeals, when an ad hoc State Supreme Court - composed of substitutes for all the justices, who could not sit on a case involving themselves — ordered the Commission's proceedings closed.

With the rest of its deliberations hidden from the public scrutiny, and with a unanimous vote needed to take any action, the Commission concluded that "no formal charges will be filed." No exoneration, no indictment. Commissioner Willoughby — Rose Bird's "valued friend" — commented about the results that, "It's not an exoneration just because we did not vote to bring charges."

Commissioner Chodos, who had withdrawn from the proceedings earlier, had predicted that the court-created obstacles to the investigation would "plant suspicion in the public mind" that the high court judges could use their vast powers to place themselves "above the law."[3]

That sorry affair was not the only example of blatant politicization of the courts under Jerry Brown.

More than fifty years ago formal standards of judicial conduct were adopted to govern the actions of California's judges. The current Code of Judicial Conduct was adopted by the Conference of California Judges and became effective on January 1, 1975. To ensure that politics was kept out of the judiciary, Cannon 7 of that Code stated that a judge "should avoid political activity which may give rise to a suspicion of political bias or impropriety."

In 1978, Mr. Jack Frankel of the Commission on Judicial Performance sent a memorandum to all California judges, entitled "Standards of Judicial Conduct." The memorandum stated that "Inasmuch as this is an election year, the Commission wishes to call particular attention to Cannon 7, which recites, A Judge Should Refrain from Political Activity Inappropriate to His Judicial Office."

On July 10, 1978, Compton Municipal Court Judge James Reese hosted a fund-raising event in his own home for the Brown for Governor campaign. The purpose was to solicit the attendance and financial support of judges. This was not a spontaneous event of which the Brown campaign was unaware. In fact, they were fully involved in the affair. Brown's judicial appointees were invited to attend. Those who did attend were pressured into purchasing tickets to a Brown fund raising dinner. These same judges and court commissioners were also asked to help sell tickets to the dinner.[4]

As crass as such Brown tactics were, they were also more than just an affront to Cannon 7. That Cannon at that time included the statement that a judge should not "solicit funds for or pay an assessment to a political organization or candidate; make contributions to a political party or organization or to a non-judicial candidate in excess of a total of one hundred dollars per year."

Among those attending the fund raising event at Judge Reese's home were: Los Angeles Municipal Court Judge Barbara Jean Johnson and David Rothman; Los Angeles Superior Court Judges Florence Bernstein (who two months later was appointed by Rose Bird to the Judicial Council), Roberta Ralph, and Vaino Spencer (who was at that time a member of the Judicial Council and who was elevated two months later to the Court of Appeal); Glendale Municipal Court Judge Lillian Stevens; Long Beach Municipal Court Judge Marcus Tucker; and several commissioners.

Judge Reese was hosting in his own home exactly the

type of political affair which judges were supposed to avoid.

Besides the Reese event, numerous judges violated the ethical Cannons during the 1978 elections by giving amounts exceeding the guidelines. Some of those judges were:[5]

Betty Barry-Deal*+ - Alameda County................ $110
Benjamin A. Diaz - Sacramento County $150
Donald B. King*+ - San Francisco County $150
Stephen Manley - Santa Clara County $150
G. Tom Thompson - Los Angeles County $200
Juaneito Vernon - Los Angeles County $250
Milton Most - Los Angeles County $350
Sherman W. Smith - Los Angeles County $200
Richard Carpeneti - San Francisco County $250
David Dolgin - City of Martinez $125
Marc Poche - Santa Clara County .,..................... $125
Carlos Rodriguez - Los Angeles County $200
Keith Sparks - Nevada County $250
Dickran Teurozian - Los Angeles County $200
Michael & Katheryn+ Todd - Los Angeles County ... $350
James Walsh - Alameda County $125
Eli Cherow - Los Angeles County $125
Leonard McLevy - Sacramento County $125
Jack M. Newman - Los Angeles County $125

*Were subsequently appointed to the California Courts of Appeals.
+Subsequently served on the Judicial Council of California.

In August of 1981 a formal complaint was filed with the Commission on Judicial Performance outlining the above offenses. On September 4, 1981, Mr. Frankel responded to that complaint by stating "Your letter was considered by the Commission at its August meeting ..... It was the decision of the Commission not to proceed further with the matter."[6] Once again, Jerry Brown's judiciary refused to investigate the transgressions of its own members. Once again, politics ruled, rather than ethics.

CHAPTER FOURTEEN

WHERE DO THEY ALL COME FROM?

One of the most difficult tasks for anyone writing about Jerry Brown's courts is that there are so many examples of poor judicial appointments that a full presentation would overwhelm the audience.

State Senator Alfred Alquist — a leading Democrat in the California State Senate — summed up the situation well. In 1979 Alquist stated, "Brown, in his second term, seems to have gone out of his way to appoint people who are extremely controversial. He's appointed so many incompetent people."[1]

Before Brown became governor, an informal system had developed to help ensure that nominees to the courts of California came from the cream of the legal profession. Lawyers under consideration for an appointment were put through a series of screening processes.

Governor Reagan, for example, required potential judicial nominees to fill out a detailed 100 question form.[2] Checks were made into personal backgrounds. Members of the legal profession — judges and lawyers — in the nominee's community were interviewed in depth concerning the nominee's competency, integrity, and personality.[3]

The reputation of California courts was built by jurists who were known for their legal scholarship and personal character. Judicial temperament — a cautious, deliberative, restrained, and dignified personality — was highly prized. It was taken for granted that judges would hold their own power in check — that their decisions would be based on solid reasoning and legal tradition — that they would adhere to a personal moral standard of the highest order.

That all changed with Jerry Brown. Brown cut the 100 question personal survey down to 38 questions. (One of the questions removed was: "Have you ever smoked marijuana?" Brown must have believed that was irrelevant — at least until his friend and judicial appointee Paul Halvonik was arrested on the dope charges in Oakland.)

When Brown was inaugurated as Governor in 1975, he promised to "open up" the appointments process — to get rid of the political hacks and to appoint the best people, regardless of sex, race, or political affiliation.

Just the opposite occurred.

James Mills, former President Pro Tem of the California State Senate - and a Democrat, aptly described the Jerry Brown system of choosing appointees. "I have seen governors appoint people who were controversial before," Senator Mills said, "but I have never seen them appoint people because they were controversial."[5]

Instead of appointing people who were best qualified, regardless of other considerations — Jerry Brown adopted a deliberate policy of choosing appointees for their political, social, ideological and sexual background and status, often regardless of legal background qualifications.

As Senator Mills commented: "There is so much emphasis on choosing representatives from various groups — blacks, browns, women — that sometimes it seems to me other considerations are neglected."[6]

But it is not the appointment of social groups under-represented in the judiciary that is the problem rather, it is the appointment of unqualified members of those groups - even when qualified persons in the same groups could have been chosen. As one judge told the *Los Angeles Times*: "I think it is clear they have appointed unqualified and barely qualified minority members ... I see every week minority lawyers more qualified than those appointed."[7]

Dan Whitehurst, the Mayor of Fresno who challenged Brown for the 1982 Democrat nomination for U.S. Senator, commented that "Jerry's appointments have exemplified what's wrong with the whole administration. Some judges were appointed almost for shock value, and some simply smack of cronyism."[8]

Two of those "shock value" appointees were chosen because of their self-professed homosexuality. On September 17, 1979, Brown appointed Steven M. Lachs to the Los Angeles County Superior Court. Lachs had run for a position on the L. A. County Municipal Court as an avowed homosexual. The voters rejected him. But Jerry Brown decided that it was time for the "gay community" to have a judge of their own. He thus appointed Lachs to a higher court than that for which the voters had defeated him.[9]

Brown decided in 1981 to be even-handed. He appointed a lesbian and member of the Alice B. Toklas Democratic Club — Mary Morgan — to the San Francisco Municipal Court.[10] (Alice B. Toklas, by the way, is a real person who has come to symbolize heavy use of marijuana.)

The Lachs/Morgan appointments were quite deliberate. Gray Davis, Brown's Chief of Staff, admitted "The Governor takes seriously the recommendations from the gay community."[11]

Of course Rose Bird is Jerry Brown's premier "shock value" appointee. Bird's legal background was conspicuously shallow. As former Appellate Court Justice George Paras commented: "I suppose I might conceive of someone in California less qualified than Rose Bird to be Chief Justice, but frankly, no one comes to mind."[12]

Bird did, however, have three qualities which appealed to Brown: she was female, a strong liberal, and was personally loyal to Brown. While Brown should not be faulted for wanting to name a woman to the California Supreme Court, the selection of an unqualified, inexperienced woman was a gratuitous insult to the many respected women judges passed over by Brown's appointment of Bird.

Even liberal activists were stunned by the Bird choice. As one stated: "A lot of people who supported Rose (in her confirmation election) out of loyalty to the institution of the court resented Jerry for appointing her when he could have found someone better qualified."[13]

But Rose Bird hasn't let Jerry Brown down in her decisions as Chief Justice. A report in the *California Journal* (February, 1981) provided a statistical profile of Bird and other Brown appointees to the Supreme Court. The report showed that Bird favored the defendant in 90 percent of the cases which concerned constitutional issues, and in 88 percent of cases involving court procedures. Bird was also the sole member of the Court to dissent on the case concerning the Proposition 13 tax cut. She argued that the tax limitation was unconstitutional — the people had no right to impose such a restriction on the government.

Bird has succinctly described her judicial views. "Justice" she said, "is when the defense wins."[14] A philosophy which is fully in keeping with her experience as a public defender.

But Bird - who had been Brown's chauffeur in his campaign for Governor, and later was a member of his administration — was not the only person appointed by Brown for political reasons. A study by the California Chamber of Commerce, published in August of 1977, showed that 97 percent of Brown's judicial appointees were Democrats.

Brown appointed his Deputy Legal Affairs Secretary, Maurice Hourdane, to the Monterey Municipal Court.[15]

He also appointed Democrat Assemblyman Bill McVittie to the Los Angeles Superior Court — even though McVittie was declared "not qualified" by the San Bernardino Bar Association for an appointment in that county.[16]

And Brown appointed a former Santa Clara County public defender — and a son of a Democrat Congressman — Leonard P. Edwards to the Santa Clara Municipal Court in 1981, even though the Santa Clara County District Attorney's Office had accused Edwards, just before his appointment, of making "false and misleading" statements in court, and had asked that Edwards be charged with contempt of court.[17]

Brown appointed other politicians to whom he owed political debts:

State Senator John Holmdahl to the Appellate Court;
State Senator George Zenovich to the Appellate Court;
State Senator Jerry Smith to the Appellate Court;
Assemblyman Eugene Gualco to the Sacramento Superior Court;
Congressman George Danielson to the Appellate Court.

He also saw to it that personal friends were taken care of by appointment to the bench, including William Newsom to the Placer County Superior Court; Marc Poche (an old friend and schoolmate from the University of Santa Clara) to the Appellate Court; and Taketsugu Takei to the Santa Clara County Superior Court.[18]

To charges of cronyism, Brown's former Legal Affairs Secretary (and now a Brown-appointed Appellate Court Judge) responded "What's wrong with appointing people that you know well?"[19]

The degree to which political considerations have come to override careful evaluation of judicial credentials was made blatantly clear when Jerry Brown appointed Milton L. McGhee to the Appellate Court.

McGhee had been Vice-Mayor of Sacramento and was

a Democrat party activist, and black — by Brown's standards, obviously sufficient for appointment to a high position in the California judicial system. Yet Brown and his staff didn't bother to send anyone to the Sacramento County Courthouse, just six blocks away from the Governor's office, to check if McGhee had any legal problems in his past. If they had, they would have found that McGhee had at least ten Superior Court civil cases filed against him for various reasons.[20] Those court records are readily available public records. Barely twenty minutes is needed to make such a simple review.

The failure to check McGhee's background created a public relations nightmare for Brown. During McGhee's confirmation hearings by the Commission on Judicial Appointments it was discovered that McGhee had been passing bad checks and was a defendant in several legal malpractice suits.[21] The State Bar Association declared McGhee as "unqualified" for the office.

An embarrassed Brown was forced to withdraw the nomination. McGhee was later indicted by the Sacramento County Grand Jury for fraud and embezzlement involving over $600,000. Some of the alleged illegal actions occurred less than a year before Brown submitted McGhee's nomination.[22]

McGhee was subsequently convicted of grand theft and sentenced to prison and disbarred. (*American Journalism Review* "Lawyers On Trial" 1992)

Commenting on the withdrawal of McGhee's nomination, Anthony Kline, Brown's Legal Secretary, stated: "We have (now) agreed with the State Bar that we will not publicly appoint anyone who has not first been found qualified by the State Bar."[23] A revolutionary idea for judicial reform!

It is Anthony Kline who is to a large degree responsible for Jerry Brown's appointments to the judiciary.

Kline met Brown when they attended Yale Law School together. Kline and Brown both moved to Berkeley, California, after law school. Brown became a clerk for the Supreme Court, while Kline opened a "public interest" law firm to use the courts to advance his liberal views. Brown, Kline and Paul Halvonik shared a car pool to their respective jobs in San Francisco.

Kline became a Director of the American Civil Liberties Union, and a leading opponent of capital punishment. When Brown became governor, he appointed his friend Anthony

Kline as Legal Affairs Secretary — giving Kline responsibility to make recommendations for judicial appointments. According to one Brown aide: "Kline made it clear from day one that if Brown allowed anyone to be executed during his term he (Kline) would quit."[24] Kline successfully wielded his influence over Brown — no death penalty sentences were carried out during Brown's administration.

As Kline said, defending Brown's judicial appointments: "Jerry Brown's position on strict enforcement of criminal laws is well-known."[25]

Quite.

Kline also commented that Brown's appointees to the judiciary would be his "greatest accomplishment," that their judges were "consistently high quality," and that "That's the legacy that is perhaps going to be his proudest achievement."[26]

If that is the case, Brown must indeed be ashamed of his years as governor.

The criticism of Brown's judicial legacy is not a result of political partisanship. One of Brown's strongest critics has been liberal Democrat and former Brown advisor, Preble Stoltz, who wrote a scathing review of Rose Bird and Brown's record of judicial appointments in his book *Judging Judges*. Stoltz is a law professor at Rose Bird's alma mater — Boalt Hall School of Law, University of California at Berkeley. He is also a former director of policy and programs for the Brown administration. Stoltz's comments serve as the background of much of the following chapters on the Bird Supreme Court.

At the end of his second term even Brown admitted his errors, of a sort. He was, he says, too insensitive to the principle of seniority in making his judicial appointments. "After eight years, I really have an acute sense that the people who have paid their dues, who have waited in line, want to be appointed. They don't want to see someone who just came along get appointed over them," Brown said.[27] Apparently Jerry Brown still doesn't recognize the damage he has truly done to the California courts.

Appellate Justice Robert Kane, who quit the bench in 1979 in public distress over the decline in the courts, said: "Jerry Brown and Tony Kline are 95 percent to blame (for the courts' problems) for avoiding experienced trial judges and putting in their inexperienced philosophical buddies."[28]

PART II

THE DECLINE
OF THE
SUPREME COURT

"MY FATHER ONCE TOLD ME, 'THE MOST IMPORTANT THING YOU DO AS GOVERNOR IS THE JUDGES YOU APPOINT. ' I'M PROUD OF EVERY ONE OF THEM."

GOVERNOR JERRY BROWN
MARCH 19, 1982
IN SACRAMENTO

CAN JUDGES WHO DO EVIL BE YOUR FRIEND? THEY DO INJUSTICE UNDER COVER OF LAW. THEY ATTACK THE LIFE OF THE JUST AND CONDEMN INNOCENT BLOOD.

PSALM 94

Never fear, my little chickadee, I'll protect you and your compatriots here from any unscrupulous vigilantes who dare to criticize you.

CHAPTER FIFTEEN

BIRD REIGNS SUPREME

In February of 1977 Governor Jerry Brown stunned the legal community by announcing the nomination of his Secretary of Agriculture and Services Agency — and his former campaign chauffeur, Rose Elizabeth Bird, to be Chief Justice of the California Supreme Court. In picking Bird to be the first woman Chief Justice, Brown passed over every experienced judge in the California judiciary — including many qualified women — choosing instead a person with no experience on the bench.

Bird's greatest qualifications were experience as a public defender and two years of teaching clinical courses in Criminal Law and Consumer Rights at Stanford.

Bird's nomination by Brown produced a pitched battle inside the California District Attorneys' Association. An effort was made to put the CDAA on record as opposed to Bird's confirmation as Chief Justice. Had that effort been successful, the Commission on Judicial Appointments (which approves or rejects a governor's nominees to the courts) might well have refused to confirm Bird.

Leading the effort in the CDAA against Bird was George Nicholson, a former executive director of the organization. On the other side was John Van de Kamp, Los Angeles County District Attorney (and, like Bird, a former Public Defender). Van de Kamp won.

"It was only through Van de Kamp's vigorous advocacy of Bird's candidacy that CDAA opposition to her was neutralized and her bare majority on the commission (on Judicial Appointments) was assured," Nicholson said after the battle. "He (Van de Kamp) injected blatant politics into the very serious business of determining whether the District Attorney's Association should oppose Rose Bird's confirmation."[1]

Born in 1936, Rose Bird graduated from Boalt Hall School of Law in 1965 — the same period when Jerry Brown, J. Anthony Kline (who became Brown's legal affairs secretary), and Paul Halvonik were living and socializing in the Berkeley area. After a year as a law clerk to the Chief Justice of the Nevada Supreme Court, Rose Bird was admitted to the California State Bar in 1966. She was hired as a Deputy Public Defender in Santa Clara County. In that office she advanced to positions as a Senior Trial Deputy and Chief of Appellate Division, Public Defender's Office.

She left her job as a public defender in 1974 to work in Jerry Brown's first campaign for Governor. Upon Brown's inauguration, she became the first woman cabinet member in California history as Secretary of Agriculture and Services.

Apparently Jerry Brown decided that personal loyalty to him was sufficient qualification to be the most powerful judge in California, the Chief Justice of the State Supreme Court. The Supreme Court, the State of California and the law haven't been the same since.

Following Jerry Brown's cue, Rose Bird moved quickly to fill key posts in the court staff — and, when she could, the courts themselves — with people personally loyal to her, or committed to the most liberal judicial philosophies.

Even before she took her oath of office, Rose Bird removed Virginia Marks — secretary and administrative aide to Chief Justices Gibson, Traynor and Wright — and Diane McHenry — the second ranking secretary to previous Chief Justices. Both of the highly qualified and experienced women were returned to the secretarial office pool.[2]

To replace Marks and McHenry, Bird hired four young lawyers (three of whom had served with her in the Santa Clara Public Defender's Office) Stephen Buehl, who became Bird's Executive Assistant, and Nicholas Selby and Richard Neuhoff, who became her research attorneys.[3]

Preble Stolz, in his book *Judging Judges*, (The Free Press, publishers) commented that Bird "apparently could not bring herself to trust people not of her own selection who might have lingering loyalties to others."

Other practices instituted by Bird were equally insulting and puzzling.

Other judges visiting with her were subjected to having their conversation transcribed by her aides — even purely social meetings. Phone calls to Bird from other judges were routinely returned not by Bird, but by her aide Stephen Buehl.[4]

Another Rose Bird habit apparently was using the "silent

treatment" toward her perceived enemies. A public investigation in 1979 of the Supreme Court's practices revealed that both Supreme Court Justices William Clark and Stanley Mosk suffered the treatment.[5]

Ralph Kleps, who had served Chief Justices well for nearly 20 years and who was Director of the Administrative Office of the court, resigned six weeks after Bird ascended to the court — in part, because Bird refused to speak to him.[6]

Bird's rude silence extended even to the career staff of Justice Clark. Clark recalled that one of his career staff members, Mr. Morris "...indicated that he had seen the chief justice in the elevator and had said good morning, and she had turned in the opposite direction without acknowledging his presence...."[7]

Before confirming her appointment as Chief Justice, the Commission on Judicial Appointments had been warned of Bird's habit and attitude toward others by a truly unimpeachable source — Roger Mahony, at that time the Catholic Bishop of Fresno. Bishop Mahony was known as being fairly liberal on social issues. He had also worked closely with Rose Bird while he served as Chairman of the Agricultural Labor Relations Board. Bird had been the prime author of the legislation creating that Board, and was at the time Brown's Secretary of Agriculture.

In a confidential letter to the Commission on Judicial Appointments, Bishop Mahony stated:[8]

> "After careful reflection I am writing to offer my vigorous opposition to (Bird's) appointment as Chief Justice, and my qualified opposition to her appointment as a Justice of the Court...
>
> "My opposition to her appointment as Chief Justice centers on her questionable emotional stability and her vindictive approach to dealing with all persons under her authority. I experienced personally her vindictiveness on many occasions when the ALRB, an independent state agency, chose to pursue a course other than that desired by Ms. Bird. She has a personal temperament which enables her to lash out at people who do not agree with her. Her normal approach is to become vindictive, then to transfer her feelings to a long phase of non-communication. She would refuse to take or return telephone calls or to acknowledge any attempts at communication.

"I am gravely concerned that the future Chief Justice of our state Supreme Court be a person of balanced emotional stability, of judicial temperament, and of correspondsible (sic) collaboration with the Justices. In my experience and opinion Ms. Bird fits none of those requirement..."

After the resignation of Ralph Kreps, Bird moved to fill that slot with another loyal ally from her days in the Santa Clara Public Defender's Office. Her choice was Ralph Gampell, the president of the California Bar Association.

Bird had passed over the court's own experienced staff, counting personal loyalty as the prime qualification.

Gampell was President of the Bar when that lawyers' organization "after considerable debate" recommended Bird's appointment to the Chief Justice position. The Bar had issued that recommendation on a split vote — 12 voting that she was qualified, and 5 abstaining. Rose's victory margin was the result of Gampell's personal efforts and vote - and that of six votes of "public members" of the Bar's Board of Governors who had just been appointed to that body by Jerry Brown. Bird had actually failed to secure the support of a majority of the lawyers on the Board of Governors of the California State Bar Association.[9]

Bird knew she could count on Gampell in the toughest situations. So she fought to have him appointed as the director of the Administrative Offices of the court. That position is filled by a vote of the entire California Judicial Council. Even though Bird, as Chief Justice, now had the power to deny reappointment to any member of the Council who dared oppose her, four of the fourteen members of the Council did so by voting against Gampell's selection to the court's chief administrative post.

One of the four was William Hogoboom, the Presiding Judge of the Los Angeles Superior Court — the largest court in the state with 171 judges. In his book, mentioned earlier, Preble Stolz observed that "The presiding judge of that court is the most important administrative figure of that court system next to the Chief Justice. To appoint Gampell over the negative vote of the presiding judge of Los Angeles Superior Court was as startling to the judiciary as if a Democratic president had appointed a Secretary of Labor over the objection of the President of the AFL-CIO."

Gampell died October 3,1988.

Hogoboom, however, seems to have been aware of the problems resulting from Bird's stewardship for the court. He had been subjected to the Bird treatment when paying a courtesy call on her, and faced Stephen Buehl taking notes of the conversation.[10]

Another key court functionary had been Jon Smock, the Sacramento lobbyist for the Judicial Council. Smock quit after some months with a strong blast at Bird. Smock's desk had been moved into a hallway and he was given no work to do.[11]

Even the press was not exempt from Bird's treatment. The *Los Angeles Times* reported in an article by Myrna Oliver "what every reporter in California has learned: the Chief Justice rarely talks to the news media, deferring all questions to aid, Stephen Buehl." Oliver also noted: "It is clear Mrs. Bird reacts in highly personal ways to anything she sees as a slight from the other justices, and that she views many things as slights."[12]

CHAPTER SIXTEEN

BIRD CONSOLIDATES HER POWER

Rose Bird wasn't content with ensuring the loyalty of her own staff. She moved quickly to surround herself with personal friends and political allies at all levels of the California court system. Possibly her reliance on known Bird loyalists was a reaction to the heavy criticism she was receiving from many quarters. Just as likely is what Connie Kang, a reporter for the *San Francisco Examiner*, concluded in an October 6, 1978 article. Kang summed up the views of the approximately 70 lawyers, judges, and court administrators whom she interviewed in preparing her article. That feeling was that most of the criticism of Bird was due to her "managing abrasively, and surrounding herself with a hand-picked, inexperienced and, in some cases, overpaid staff of loyal followers."

The Chief Justice, among other positions of power, serves as the Chairman of the Judicial Council. There are 21 members on the Council — 14 of whom are appointed by the Chief Justice. Four others are appointed by the State Bar, one by the President of the State Senate, and one by the Speaker of the Assembly. Through the Judicial Council, the Chief Justice controls the administration of the courts, adopts and implements rules and forms, and holds the power to temporarily assign judges between courts or to a higher court.

As Paul Haerle, a distinguished San Francisco lawyer, remarked in a letter published in the *California Journal*: "... Chief Justice Bird controls all of the judges in California from justice courts to Supreme Court and without statutory accountability."

In that letter, Haerle continued to describe the powers which Bird had assumed: "Another consequence of the Bird appointment, however, harbors even further potential for control of the judicial system. ...(former) Chief Justice

Wright appointed retired Superior Court Judges pro tempore to fill the vacancies (on the Court of Appeal), a felicitous device which results in the employment of good judicial talent at little expense or inconvenience. This practice has been abrogated by Chief Justice Bird. Now ... sitting Superior Court Judges are to be selectively elevated for four — to six — week periods. These pro tem appointees do not, of course have the independence of appointed justices or retired judges. Although the practice may give trial judges more rounded perspective, they are necessarily under some pressure to please in order to be permanently appointed, or at least selected for a further term of apprenticeship.

"Moreover, ... such sitting Superior Court Judges must be replaced ... by the temporary elevation of a municipal court judge, who, in turn, can be replaced by a lawyer willing to try a few weeks on the other side of the bench. Thus, for every appellate court vacancy temporarily filled there can be three or more judicial hopefuls beholden to the Governor and to the Chief Justice every four to six weeks."

Before Bird there had been a formal delegation of authority to the chief administrator of the Supreme Court to manage the assignment function with the sole objective of getting the job done. Bird undertook to make the decisions herself. She also established a policy of assigning retired judges only to lower courts than they had previously served — superior court judges to serve on municipal courts, for example.[1]

Elevate the less experienced and demote the old hands seemed to be Rose Bird's attitude.

Some observers have remarked that Bird's policies looked suspiciously like patronage to her followers and like a method of screening judges for possible future promotion.

The extent to which Bird had sought control over the court system is made clear by her policy on the appellate departments of superior courts. Those departments hear appeals from the municipal courts in the respective counties - misdemeanor cases.

The power to appoint the three judge appellate panels in every county rests with the Chief Justice. But the last three chief justices have allowed the presiding judges of the larger counties to make their own appointments. Bird established a system of only asking for the recommendations of the presiding judges — which she then regularly rejects. Instead, she has chosen judges already assigned to other duties, thus disrupting the judicial processes and requiring reassignment of other judges to fill vacancies created.[2]

Rose Bird's first appointments to the Judicial Council were not made until February 1, 1978. She had been appointed and confirmed as Chief Justice too late in 1977 to make the two year appointments which were up at the time.

Bird chose Supreme Court Justice Wiley Manuel (a Jerry Brown appointee and a Democrat), Appeals Court Judge Bernard Jefferson (a Jerry Brown Democrat), Appeals Court Judge Stephen Tamura (a Pat Brown appointee and a Democrat, although Reagan had designated him as Presiding Judge of his court), Superior Court Judge Richard Abbe (a Pat Brown Democrat), Superior Court Judge Spurgeon Avakian (a Pat Brown appointee and one of the only two former members of the Judicial Council reappointed by Bird), Superior Court Judge Harry Low (a Democrat, he had won election in San Francisco on his own, but Reagan did appoint him to fill a seven-month vacancy until his own term began), Superior Court Judge Richard Schauer (a Pat Brown Republican), Superior Court Judge Vaino H. Spencer (a Jerry Brown Democrat), Municipal Court Judge Ann Marie Chargin (a Jerry Brown appointee), Municipal Court Judge Lewis Wenzell (a Jerry Brown appointee), and Justice Court Judges Rick Brown and Vivian Quinn.

When Bird took office, there were on the Judicial Council five Pat Brown appointees, five Reagan appointees, one who had been appointed by Brown and elevated by Reagan, one Jerry Brown appointee, and two Justice Court Judges appointed by their respective County Board of Supervisors. Where political party affiliation was known, there were seven Democrats and five Republicans. In all, a fair political and judicial balance.

Bird's appointments heavily tilted the Council towards her own political party and philosophy. Five had been appointed to the judiciary by Jerry Brown, six by Pat Brown and none by Reagan. Of her eight appointees, seven were Democrats and only one was a Republican.

Besides the Judicial Council there is another important arm of the California court system — the Commission on Judicial Performance. The Commission is the disciplinary arm of the courts and was created by the state constitution as an independent state agency with a wide scope of powers. It

94

can take actions ranging from privately admonishing a judge for a minor offense, to recommending to the Supreme Court that a judge be publicly censured or even removed from office.

While supposedly independent, the rules which govern the Commission are established by the Judicial Council — making the Commission functionally a subsidiary of the Council.

The members of the Commission are appointed by the Supreme Court. The Commission consists of two Appeals Court judges, two Superior Court judges, one Municipal Court judge, two appointees of the Bar, and two "public members" appointed by the Governor.

When Bird became Chief Justice the Commission had a balance of two Reagan judges, two Pat Brown judges and one judge who had been appointed by Governor Knight.

Because the members serve staggered four year terms, Bird was able to make her first appointment in 1977. She chose John T. Racanelli, a personal friend who had testified at Bird's confirmation hearings.[3] Racanelli had been appointed to the bench by Pat Brown, and was elevated by Jerry Brown. He was, of course, a registered Democrat.

Connie Kang's October 6, 1978 article in the *San Francisco Examiner* revealed that Bird had appointed Racanelli to the Commission without bothering to obtain the concurrence of the other members of the Supreme Court. The state constitution specifically gives the appointment power to the court as a whole — not to the Chief Justice.

In 1978, Bird appointed Los Angeles Superior Court Judge Jerry Pacht — a pedigreed ACLU Liberal Democrat — to fill out a vacancy. Pacht once ran for partisan office as a Democrat with the support of the Committee for Liberal Representation — a "new left" group of Democrat Party activists including now-Congressman Howard Berman.

In 1979 Bird appointed Pacht to a full four-year term and appointed Appeals Court Justice Robert O. Staniforth — another Jerry Brown Democrat — to fill another seat on the Commission.

In 1980, Bird appointed then-Superior Court Judge Allen Broussard to the Commission — another Jerry Brown Democrat, later named as a Justice of the California Supreme Court by Brown. In 1981 Bird selected Superior Court Judge Richard Bancroft — a Jerry Brown Democrat — and Municipal

Court Judge Charles Coff — a Democrat from San Francisco who had been appointed to the court by Reagan.

By 1981 the Commission was composed of three Jerry Brown appointed judges, and one Pat Brown judge, and one Reagan-appointed judge. All four who listed their party in their biographies were Democrats.

Either Chief Justice Rose Bird believed that there are no qualified Republican judges on the California court bench, or she was determined to stack the system with her personal and political allies. It is a curious coincidence that Rose Bird and Jerry Brown argue that critics of their control of the courts are opposed to "an independent judiciary" —while Bird and Brown have made political allegiance a clear pre-requisite for appointment to the court system.

CHAPTER SEVENTEEN

CRACKING THE WHIP - SELECTIVELY

When Rose Bird assumed her position as Chief Justice of the California Supreme Court, she put out the word that she would not tolerate slowness by California judges. She announced that all judges would be required to adhere to the 90-day rule. That rule, which is part of the California State Constitution, mandates that judges decide cases within 90 days of the case being submitted to the court, or the judge will lose all pay until the case is decided.

The enforcement of the rule is both legally required, and commendable - provided it is not imposed selectively.

Bird didn't have to wait long to prove she meant business. In 1978 the Commission on Judicial Performance recommended to the Supreme Court that it censure Santa Barbara Superior Court Judge Arden T. Jensen (a Reagan appointee) for failure to decide cases in a timely manner.

The Supreme Court voted to follow the recommendation and censured Judge Jensen. But they stated in their decision that the "failure to decide his cases on time was not caused by an intentional disregard of his duties, but that with proper application he could have decided each of the matters within 90 days of submission..."

Bird established to the court system that she was in charge and that there would be no disregard of the rules tolerated in California courts.

Unless, of course, the rules are disregarded by Bird herself and her Supreme Court colleagues.

The year following Judge Jensen's censure, the Law and Order Campaign Committee (LOCC) filed suit in Sacramento Superior Court charging that the California Supreme Court itself had approximately 90 cases which violated the 90-days rule. LOCC asked the Superior Court to take action under Article 6, Section 19 of the California Constitution which requires withholding of all pay from judges who fail to meet the 90-day time limit for decisions.[1]

The LOCC suit, technically, was brought against State Controller Ken Cory to bar him from issuing paychecks to the high court judges. Since a private citizens' group was suing a state official, the California Attorney General's Office represented Cory - and, indirectly, the Supreme Court Justices.

On September 27, 1979, Sacramento Superior Court Judge Joseph Babich issued a temporary injunction against Cory preventing him from paying the judges' salaries. Addressing the Court, Judge Babich said that the 90-day rule was based on "a theory according to the Bible, that if you don't work, you don't eat." Judge Babich himself had once been recognized by the ACLU for ensuring speedy trials in his court back when that was fashionable.

Cory was stunned by the decision and was unsure if he would appeal the case. Deputy Attorney General Susan Underwood was surprised and challenged Babich's decision on when a case is legally considered to be submitted.

Babich had ruled that "a matter is submitted when the court has heard all arguments, or has approved a waiver of all arguments, and the time has passed for filing all briefs and papers, including any supplementary briefs permitted by the court." That ruling was the key to the decision.

The California State Constitution does not define when a case is considered submitted to the Supreme Court. Those representing Bird and her fellow Court members contended that a case was not submitted until the Court was ready to file its opinion. In other words, Birdian legal logic interpreted the Constitution as saying that the Court has 90 days to issue a decision after the day the court makes its decision.

The Bird Supreme Court had thus wanted to adopt one definition of the 90 day rule for lower courts, and another, almost meaningless rule, for itself.

The cases involved in the LOCC suit which the Supreme Court held for more than 90 days ranged from extremely important ones to those characterized as "simply a poor devil sitting in a jail cell." One case, involving an indigent roofer waiting for a possible multi-million dollar award, had been held by the Supreme Court for over 900 days![2]

After mulling the situation over, Controller Cory said that if the Justices wanted the decision overturned they could appeal the Babich decision themselves but that he probably wouldn't. After all, Cory said: "its their rights that are being trampled upon."[3] However, within a month Cory was under tremendous and mounting political pressure from Jerry Brown's allies to appeal the decision.

Even before such an appeal, however, the LOCC suit was having its intended results. The excessive backlog had taken a big fall to 31 cases past 90 days. (Although there were still at least 9 which had been before the Court for over a year.) With their paychecks being withheld, the Bird Court was making great progress catching up with its case-load.

Not all the Justices of the Supreme Court disagreed with the 90-day rule. Justice William Clark publicly argued that the rule was proper, that the court shouldn't receive its pay until it had caught up with the work it had.

Of course, Rose Bird didn't like such comments from her fellow Justices. In testimony during a later investigation of the Supreme Court's procedures by the Commission on Judicial Performance, Bird objected to Clark's comments as a personal affront to her. "...I thought it was done," she said, "not to personally just bother me within the court but to demean me in the eyes of the public."[4]

We could not expect Bird and her associates to adopt the same principled policy of an earlier California Supreme Court which, in 1911, ordered its own salary withheld when it fell behind on the ninety-day rule.

The Bird side of the LOCC case was financed, of course by the limitless resources of the state. LOCC, which was defending the rights of the taxpayers and litigants, had to finance its own legal actions. With the State Supreme Court prodded into more rapid decisions, and with its own funds running out, LOCC decided to drop the case.

WE TAKE CARE OF OUR OWN

Bird's advancement of her political and philosophical allies wasn't restricted to the Supreme Court's staff — but extended to the court's bench and its decisions.

In February of 1982, the California judicial system was stunned by press revelations of partisanship by the state's Supreme Court. The *Sacramento Union* summed up the charges with the headline: "Bird Almost Always Plugs Court Vacancies With Liberals."[1] The Union editorially called it: "Another black eye for the state Supreme Court."[2]

The article by Bob Egelko reported that in the five years she had been on the court, Chief Justice Rose Bird had used her constitutional power to fill temporary vacancies on the California Supreme Court to appoint liberals who would side with her in most cases.

The Chief Justice annually fills hundreds of vacancies on lower courts with little, if any, public attention. However, appointments to the seven member Supreme Court - even if temporary — can have a wide and lasting impact due to the precedents set by the court. By February of 1982, Bird had filled over 200 temporary vacancies in the Supreme Court, according to Egelko. These Bird appointments have had a profound impact on California law and politics.

It was a Bird appointee, retired Appeals Court Justice Stephen Tamura, who gave Bird the critical fourth vote in the Court's January 1982 4 to 3 decision on legislative reapportionment. That decision held that: (1) the 1982 elections would take place in districts reapportioned by the Democrat controlled legislature; (2) the referenda to throw out the gerrymandered reapportionment, and which under state law should have stayed implementation of the reapportionment bill would have no such effect.

The purpose of a referendum under California law is to halt the imposition of laws which a large number of citizens find objectionable until the voters of the state can decide the issue. In the state Supreme Court's decision on the reapportionment issue, Bird and her cohorts argued that a minority of the people (the hundreds of thousands of ordinary citizens who signed the reapportionment referenda petitions) should not be allowed to thwart the will of all the people as expressed through the legislature. That, of course, is a direct contradiction of the very purpose of having the referendum procedure.

The referenda repealing the reapportionment were passed by the voters of California on June 8, 1982 by 2 to 1 margins. Despite the overwhelming expression of the true will of the people, however, the blatantly partisan gerrymandering would still be in effect for the 1982 elections.

The Bird court's decision is made even more clearly partisan because it ignored a State Constitutional Amendment passed by a vote of the people in 1980. Known as Proposition 6, that amendment was intended to end the greatest abuses of reapportionment by prohibiting unnecessary division of cities, counties, and other geographical areas. The amendment was drafted by Democrat Assemblyman Jim Keysor and passed the State Legislature with bipartisan support. However, after it was passed, and before it was placed on the ballot for a vote of the people, the Democratic leadership in the Legislature decided that good government and good politics don't mix. They launched an unsuccessful effort to remove the proposal from the ballot.

In 1981 the Democrat-dominated legislature, without public hearings — or even publicly-released maps of the proposed new districts — hastily passed artfully-drawn new reapportionment lines. During the reapportionment battle in Sacramento, Democrat Congressman Phil Burton, who had personally designed the new congressional lines, told his fellow congressmen that, as far as reapportionment was concerned: "L.A. (Los Angeles) is dog meat..." (*California Magazine*, November, 1981). Apparently Rose Bird agreed.

The public reaction was so strong that nearly one million signatures were gathered on the referenda petitions.

In response to Bob Egelko's article, Rose Bird's chief aide, Stephen Buehl, charged that the report was politically motivated. Buehl denied that Bird's appointments were biased. "She's tried to give everybody an opportunity to sit (on the court) and that's what's happened," said Buehl.[3]

An unbiased review of the facts, however, makes Buehl's

claim of unbiased appointments doubtful at best.

On at least eight occasions Rose Bird named the very liberal Third District Court of Appeals Justice Cruz Reynoso to fill vacancies on the Supreme Court. Yet, she never once appointed the conservative Presiding Justice of the same Appeals Court, Justice Robert Puglia. Bird also never selected another conservative of the Third District Appeals Court, Justice Hugh Evans. And she had appointed a third conservative on that Appeals Court bench, Justice George Paras, only once — and then to hear a minor State Bar disciplinary case.[4] Bird did, however, appoint the other strong liberal from the Third District, Justice Coleman Blease on several occasions.[5]

"Maybe we don't measure up to her high standards of scholarship" Puglia complained, "or perhaps we're lacking in the amount of judicial experience which she feels is necessary to sit on the Supreme Court."[6]

That is unlikely, since Justices Puglia, Evans and Paras all had served longer on the Appeals Court than Reynoso or Blease — longer, in fact, than Bird had served on the Supreme Court, the only judgeship she had ever held.

Paras, a tough critic of Bird and Reynoso, is now retired from the bench and was one of President Reagan's appointees to the U.S. Legal Services Corporation Board of Directors. Paras criticized Bird's Supreme Court assignments as "an incredible exhibition of politicking."[7]

Bernard Jefferson, another liberal Appeals Court Justice, was appointed 16 times by Bird. Retired Appeals Court Justice Wakefield Taylor, a moderate, was appointed more than ten times. Other liberals who regularly served as Bird appointees to the Supreme Court include Joseph Rattigan, Joseph Grodin, Clinton White (of whom we have written about earlier in this book), and John Racanelli (as of early 1982).[8]

Bird seldom, if ever, appointed such conservative Appeals Court Justices as Robert Thompson, Robert Kane, Macklin Fleming, L. Thaxton Hanson, or Robert Gardner.[9] In fact, these and other highly qualified and highly regarded jurists, were pointedly passed over when Bird made dubious judicial history by selecting a liberal municipal court judge (Auerbach) to sit pro tem on the California Supreme Court.

A study published by the Stanford Law Review in 1980 analyzed the temporary appointments of the last four Chief Justices of the California Supreme Court. The study covered the period from 1954 to mid-1979, and dealt only with close cases in which there were at least two dissenting votes and in which temporary Supreme Court appointees were involved.[10]

The study found that not since Phil Gibson was Chief Justice eighteen years ago has a Chief Justice appointed temporary justices who agreed more often with the Chief Justice than has Rose Bird. Bird's appointees sided with her 80% of the time. Gibson's appointees agreed with him 85% of the time. Chief Justice Roger Traynor won such agreement in only 52% of the cases studied, and Chief Justice Donald Wright had only 75% agreement from his appointees.

Ralph Kleps was a long-time career Chief Administrative Officer of the California Courts until his resignation shortly after Bird's appointment. Kleps contended that Wright and Traynor "made a deliberate effort to rotate the assignments so nobody could make the assertion that the assignments were for the purpose of influencing the outcome."[11]

The effect of Bird's partisan appointment of less qualified temporary Supreme Court Justices was made clear in the famous 1977 Caudillo case. In that case Bird and her allies on the court ruled that multiple forced rape, sodomy, and oral copulation do not constitute great bodily harm.

Bird assigned the task of writing the majority opinion to her pro tem appointee, Justice Bernard Jefferson. Jefferson's 23 page opinion included a graphic account of each act involved in the case. But that attention to detail didn't appear in his legal presentation. He mistakenly deleted the key word on which the whole case turned. When Caudillo was convicted the California Statutes used the word bodily - which could include mental or emotional damage. Jefferson, in his written opinion, substituted the word physical, which was not used in the California Statute until ten years after Caudillo's conviction. What is even worse legal scholarship was that Jefferson used the language of a 1977 amendment to the statute which the legislature enacted, but then repealed before it went into effect.

This was an opinion in which Bird and her fellow Supreme Court Justices Tobriner, Mosk and Manuel concurred without dissent. Justices Clark and Richardson disagreed, stating that: "even assuming that something more 'substantial' than rape is required to constitute great bodily harm, surely that test is satisfied in the present case."[12]

CHAPTER NINETEEN

CHANGING LEGAL HISTORY — NOW YOU SEE IT, NOW YOU DON'T

No single California Supreme Court practice stirs the ire of more prosecutors, confuses more attorneys and divides more judges than the depublishing of appellate opinions.

Depublishing is the procedure by which the Supreme Court removes from the law books the decisions of appeals courts. An appeals court decision is the law of the state throughout the appellate district, unless, of course, it is overturned by the State Supreme Court on appeal. Those decisions also serve as precedent in other jurisdictions. The use of such precedents helps ensure uniformity of the law throughout California.

But the California Supreme Court can remove from the body of the laws decisions with which it doesn't agree — and without a formal ruling on the issues involved — simply by depublishing the appellate opinions.

In one case in 1978, In re Michael C. 21 Cal. 3rd 471, a decision by the Supreme Court itself was ordered depublished by the Bird Court.

In the past five years under Rose Bird, the California Supreme Court has been using the practice with increasing frequency. Some prosecutors and judges charge that it is being used as a form of censorship to strike down legal opinions with which the Supreme Court disagrees, but which it is unwilling to consider on appeal and overturn.

The power to depublish comes from a 1964 rule adopted by the California Supreme Court, Rule 976. The rule was originally adopted in response to California attorneys who argued that not all appeals court cases needed to be published — since they do not all add anything new to the law but simply restate earlier opinions.

Rule 976 required that opinions which were to be published must: (1) set new law; (2) involve an issue of continuing public interest; or (3) criticize existing law. To enforce these provisions the State Supreme Court granted itself the power to depublish decisions not conforming to these standards.

At first, the Supreme Court used the rule sparingly. For example, the Advance Sheet (the first publication of opinions) for July 1, 1971, shows only one case depublished without further action.

The use of the depublishing "tool" increased in 1972 and 1973, but declined in 1974 and 1975. The July 1975 Advance Sheets show only 5 cases depublished.

Depublishing grew drastically from 1976 on — under Rose Bird's regime. In April 1976, the Advance Sheets showed 150 cases depublished.

The complaints against depublishing are not limited to the frequency of the practice. There are also strong allegations of censorship against the Supreme Court. The harshest criticism comes from career prosecutors. These prosecutors charge that the Court was selectively using depublication to strike out appellate court decisions which would make prosecution of criminals easier.

It might be argued that in depublishing these opinions, the court is simply following the law (its own self-imposed Rule 976), and the decertified cases do not meet the criteria of that Rule. But the prominent murder case of People v. Level makes that argument suspect.

The issue in Level was not whether a suspect had been read his rights — he had — but whether he had "indicated" in some manner that he did not want to be questioned. After a suspect has "indicated" his wish to remain silent, even a freely-given confession is considered to have been obtained under duress, and therefore is inadmissible evidence.

In Level the Court of Appeal (102 Cal. App 3rd 897), on a two to one vote, overturned the murder conviction of Willie Edward Level. The court majority held that, once Level expressed a desire to have his mother present for his confession, the interviewing officer should have halted his questioning. The court also said that it was a violation of Level's Miranda rights (to remain silent) for the officer to suggest to Level that his confession might be embarrassing to him in front of his mother.

On April 30, 1980, the California Supreme Court denied a hearing in the case. On December 8, 1980, the United

States Supreme Court struck down the Appeals Court decision and returned the case to the California Court of Appeals. That court then unanimously affirmed Level's conviction. On June 25, 1981, the California Supreme Court denied a hearing, but ordered the Level case depublished.

In effect, the state Supreme Court was saying that the earlier, published, opinion of the Appeals Court — which had overturned Level's conviction — was good law. And the ordered depublication implied that, as far as the California Supreme Court was concerned, the opinion affirming the conviction was bad law. This kind of censorship is the reason so many observers of the California Supreme Court have charged it with using Rule 976 as a tool to undermine the prosecution of criminals.

In another case, People v. Madrigal, the California Court of Appeal unanimously affirmed the conviction for sale of heroin. But in a separate concurring opinion, Presiding Justice George Paras charged that the "Supreme Court has in the past few years, with ever expanding appetite, abused its depublication power by ordering appellate opinions depublished even though irrefutable within the standards for publication. This is often done without a single vote in favor or the grant of a hearing (by the Supreme Court), thereby indicating unanimous approval of the legal soundness and validity of the decision in question (cf. Cal. Rules of Court, Rule 29); such depublication therefore denotes an obvious dislike for the decision's rule of law and an unwillingness to let it serve as legal precedent ... We have certified the foregoing opinion for publication in the Official Reports because it meets the standards for publication as set forth in Rule 976(b). Specifically, it 'establishes a new rule of law or alters or modifies an existing rule.' But I have reason to believe that the subject matter, along with the result we reached will not be to our Supreme Court's liking, thus triggering a grant of a hearing, or more likely, depublication. If the former, I have no complaint; if the latter, I respectfully inform the Supreme Court of my disapproval. If the Court disagrees with our holding, let it grant a hearing and decide the case according to its wisdom and duty. But if it is not inclined to do so, I entreat it to discontinue the practice I here denounce."

Justice Paras' plea fell on deaf ears. The California Supreme Court ordered the case depublished.

FROM THE CALIFORNIA OFFICIAL REPORTS

Official Advance Sheet of Supreme Court, Courts of Appeal, and Appellate Departments of the Superior Courts - published by Bancroft-Whitney Co.

Cumulative Subsequent History Table

Number of cases certified for non-publication by order of the California Supreme Court.

Number 19	July 1, 1971	1 case
Number 18	July 5, 1972	10 cases
Number 18	July 5, 1973	19 cases
Number 19	July 9, 1974	14 cases
Number 18	July 1, 1975	5 cases (3 criminal)
Number 19	July 13, 1976	22 cases (6 criminal)
Number 18	July 5, 1977	21 cases (7 criminal)

In 1977, Rose Bird was confirmed as Chief Justice.

Number 18	July 6, 1978	38 cases (16 criminal)
Number 19	July 10, 1979	33 cases (16 criminal)
Number 18	July 1, 1980	68 cases (29 criminal)
Number 18	July 2, 1981	89 cases (48 criminal)
Number 9	April 1, 1982	150 cases (84 criminal)

PART III

VOICES FOR RESTORATION OF THE COURTS

"JUDGES, AS PERSONS, OR COURTS AS INSTITUTIONS, ARE ENTITLED TO NO GREATER IMMUNITY FROM CRITICISM THAN OTHER PERSONS OR INSTITUTIONS...JUDGES MUST BE KEPT MINDFUL OF THEIR LIMITATIONS AND OF THEIR ULTIMATE PUBLIC RESPONSIBILITY...BY A VIGOROUS STREAM OF CRITICISM...EXPRESSED WITH CANDOR...HOWEVER BLUNT!"

THE LATE SUPREME COURT
JUSTICE FELIX FRANKFURTER

JERRY BROWN REDUX: ONCE BITTEN, TWICE SHY, OR HOW THE PROGRESSIVE IDEOLOGICAL PROMISE OF A NEW TERM BY GOV. MOONBEAM IS AN ACT OF LUNACY

By Micah Van Zandt

In the current political epoch, ideology is perhaps more con-spicuous than it ever has been. It is also more central to the consideration of the thinking, voting citizen than ever before. Edmund G. (Jerry) Brown, the Moonbeam, has returned to vie for Governor of California once more. A progressive prodigal to some, he seeks a third term and doubtless a fourth if all goes well and the electorate is sufficiently som-nambulant or amnesiac. Why he seeks to run, at his ad-vanced age, and on demonstrably failed policies is anyone's guess. Perhaps it's to secure some obscure legacy, or simple ego. In any event, the prospect is ominous and dangerous: dangerous to our freedom, our safety, our families, and our free enterprise system.

As a man and a politician, like President Obama, Jerry Brown is an unabashed progressive. A man like Jerry Brown could be said to be a mentor to modern progressives, and to someone like an Obama. This label should not be understood as an innocuous euphemism, but rather in its correct, origi-nal sense. The term "progressive" refers to people who seek to undermine and destroy the current society in order to replace it with a society where the individual is subservient to the collective. That collective is managed by the govern-ment. Where we cherish, or purport to, individual freedoms to think, to worship, to profit, to pursue happiness, the pro-gressive champions social justice and seeks any means, fair or foul, to that end. Among the time-honored tactics of the progressives has been to undermine the courts, the criminal justice system in particular.

This was the area where the erstwhile Gov. Brown was most effective. Crime in California was more than rampant in the late 1970's and early 1980's, and rather than act decisively to protect the public, or to recognize the victims of crime, Brown moved swiftly to appoint a plethora of toxic judges, culminating in the ludicrous appointment of Rose Bird to preside over California's Supreme Court. Bird was perhaps the most unqualified person ever to sit on a high court anywhere, but bad as her appointment was, even more damage was done by Brown in the trial and lower appellate courts. An amazing number of outright incompetent, corrupt, or unqualified persons were appointed by Brown to the bench at all levels. The anecdotes about these bad judges are legion. The damage they did was epic.

As you go through this book, gentle reader, you will likely recoil at what Jerry Brown did. You will likely be aghast at the extent of the damage. You will also likely be uplifted by the successful responses of an outraged public. Most of his appointments went to people who frankly shared his ideology. A basic tenet of that ideology, among others, is that the system as envisioned by our Founders is an anachronistic vestige of elite oligarchs. The Jerry Browns of the world believe the system was set up to benefit a ruling class of Northern European-descended male capitalists, and everybody else be damned. They hold this view despite the weight of history, and the very words of the Constitution the Founders agonized to draft.

Our system was developed not to benefit rulers, but to benefit everyone. Rulers in the form of kings, dictators, or mobs (i.e., "the collective") were regarded with great suspicion by the Founders. Fail-safes were built in, the so-called "checks and balances," because the Founders were well aware of the evil people were capable of, and that of people seeking or possessing power in particular. Also, built into the Constitution was a way to amend it when or if circumstances warranted it. However, rather than follow the law, people like Jerry Brown simply ignore it and find a way to the end they seek.

Jerry Brown's tenure as Governor is a clear example of ends justifying means. Because he could not achieve through normal, legal processes the results he sought, he simply found other ways. By appointing judges who shared his ideology, he found an effective method for circumventing the rule of law, to get the result he wanted. Ironic, considering judges are supposed to be the arbiters of and the very symbols for the rule of law. Unfortunately, the effect on public safety was catastrophic, as you will read. Ultimately, because things were so bad, the public rose up and turned on Brown and Bird, passing landmark legislation known as Propositions 8 and 115, and throwing out the activist upper echelon of the California Supreme Court, Chief Justice Bird and company.

A short explanation of Propositions 8 and 115 is in order. These initiatives essentially undid many of the activist rulings by the Brown judiciary, which was openly and unapologetically legislating from the bench. The Proposition 8 referred to in this article is not to be confused with the recent Prop 8 just voted on concerning homosexual marriages. The older Prop 8 established the Crime Victim's Bill of Rights, among other things, placing it in the California Constitution (Article I, section 28(b)). Crime victims were no longer relegated to suffering in silence while their criminal victimizers were being granted unprecedented rights. Victims now had the right to be heard on the impact of criminal acts on their lives. They had the right to be protected from intimidation, to notice from the courts and prosecution about hearings, to have their personal information be secure, and to restitution from the criminal for losses they incurred. It was then, and remains, a major piece of legislation, imitated around the country.

Proposition 115 was passed to correct the numerous hyper-technical rulings from the bench that significantly altered the criminal procedure and evidence landscapes. The Brown-stacked courts were simply changing long-standing rules of evidence and court to favor criminals, as you will see below. It was very difficult to prosecute anything but the most straightforward crimes. Search and seizure law was turned on its head. Previously admissible statements by criminals and witnesses were suddenly inadmissible. Warrants were required for searches that never required them before. Dangerous and violent offenders were routinely released on the most slender pretexts. It was an uphill fight for a prosecutor to get the necessary probable cause just to hold a criminal to answer for a crime, much less a conviction.

The main agenda of the Bird-Brown court was to maximally extend the rights of the accused beyond anything ever contemplated, and far beyond the protections already guaranteed in the Federal Constitution (Bird herself was a former Public Defender, and never sat as a judge on any bench before her appointment to the state's highest court). This came at the expense of public safety, obviously, as it became virtually impossible to prosecute all but the most open-and-shut criminal cases. Jails truly had revolving doors, and often the defendant simply walked out of court, never going to jail at all. Victims, and their rights, were completely ignored, and if the subject was somehow brought up, victims and their "rights" were marginalized or even mocked.

Of course, the public refused to stand for it. The media in those days still did a passable job reporting the actual news, and the main topic was usually about crime. Horrific crimes were center stage daily, and there was plenty of coverage about the outrages by the courts. The Bird Court was philosophically opposed to the death penalty and simply decided it would not enforce the law. The Bird court found any excuse to overturn a capital verdict, flatly refusing to comply with the existing law, as was their sworn duty to uphold and apply. The chapters below explore these travesties in detail.

Bad as openly flouting the law in capital cases was, worse still was the carnage wrought in the areas of search and seizure and suspect statements/confessions (corrected in large measure by Prop 115). Police and prosecutors were seriously hampered, as noted above, because so much of any potential case could be thrown out by the courts, even if law enforcement did everything completely properly. This was because the courts were making new rules of criminal procedure and evidence out of whole cloth to the benefit of criminals. Guilt, even where obvious, was not a consideration. Mayhem was the inevitable result. The reign of the Red Queen was in full flower.

The electorate reacted, as noted, by tossing out the worst judges and by passing Props 8 and 115, which undid the criminal-friendly case law the courts created. Yes, the courts appointed themselves legislators, and simply crafted the law to get the social justice oriented result sought. Fortunately, the People still had recourse in the voter initiatives that made it to the ballot and were resoundingly passed.

Unfortunately, many legislators in the state had abdicated their duty to the courts, apparently comfortable to let the black-robed minions do their work for them.

Of course, not all judges and legislators were on board with this lunacy. Most who took their charge seriously vigorously fought Jerry Brown and his appointees. Primarily because of the dedicated public servants actually heeding their sworn duties, Prop's 8 and 115 were drafted, vetted, and placed before the voters. These men and women are heroes, champions of public safety and the rule of law. Please read their stories below and remember their names as true public servants.

The Jerry Brown era, circa 1975-1983, has begun to recede into memory. He is cultivating a false image as an elder-statesman now, hoping most will not recall, or ever learn about his legacy as Governor. After being Governor, he tried repeatedly to become the President of the U.S., and was repeatedly rejected. Not to be left out of the public trough, he eventually became the mayor of Oakland, and recently had an unproductive stint as California's Attorney General. Unfortunately, the term limit law of 1990 apparently failed to contemplate a situation like the return of Brown, and so here is he is, ready to extend the legacy of lunacy.

Nothing from 1983 to now indicates he has changed his ideology one iota, to borrow a turn of phrase from Edward Gibbon (*The History of the Decline and Fall of the Roman Empire*, Strahan & Cadell, London, 1788). It would be interesting to read an evaluation of the decline and fall of California, and of leaders like Jerry Brown, written by someone with Gibbon's insight and keen analysis. That shall remain a pleasing fantasy. Happily, there are plenty of excellent writings out there analyzing Brown's shortcomings as Governor, such as the one you are about to read. The height of folly would be to re-elect him now, in a dismal economy, with empty public coffers, and permit him to resume his wrecking of judiciary, particularly now that he has the value of hindsight. Who believes he has had any sea-change in his thinking? The risk is too great to find out.

A New Age of governance by the Lunar One portends an erosion of public safety, first and foremost. Such an age would not be the "Age of Aquarius." Brown most certainly would seek to reinstate his policies and appoint like-minded people to accomplish this. He prided himself on ignoring the

People, the voters, as well as the law, and now he wants a "redux." What we need is a reckoning to recall and tally the damage he did, and to repel him from ever taking power in this state again. We need to remind the electorate about the real danger he poses. The last thing the beleaguered voters of this state need is to return to the grim daily reality of fear and danger from rising crime rates, particularly in this bad economy. Does anyone believe he will not seek to undermine any portion of the gains cemented by Prop's 8 and 115?

An insight into his thinking, into his ultimate purpose, is instructive. We have to understand the core beliefs of a Jerry Brown. Predictably, Brown, like Obama, will want to stick his fingers into, change, and control everything we as free people believe in, and in everything we do. Brown and Obama are progressive extremists, no overstatement here. Neither man believes in free enterprise, or for that matter, our freedoms. To paraphrase Winston Churchill, both see private enterprise as a predatory target to be shot and as a cow to be milked. Further, by undermining the criminal justice system with activist judges, it is increasingly impossible to protect our private property and enterprises. The goal is, of course, to encourage the collapse of the current system in order to facilitate its replacement by one more to the collectivist/progressivist liking. They do not see the free enterprise system as the "sturdy horse" pulling the wagon.

Neither Brown, nor Obama for that matter, has ever created a single private-sector job. Neither one is interested now in fostering private-sector job creation and growth, nor are they interested in helping reduce unemployment in California, or the nation at large. Both, as noted, are committed progressive left-wing extremists. Among other methods, like besieging the courts, "leaders" like these use the cause of environmentalism to undermine the free enterprise economy. No rational person wants a poisoned environment or species going extinct, but the goal of the so-called environmentalists in collaboration with progressives in power is not a cleaner world burgeoning with wildlife with sustainable power, but rather to destroy the existing system. This is accomplished by byzantine laws and regulations, both state and federal that dismember this state's and the nation's capacities to produce, protect, and preserve wealth and create jobs. This malevolent effort will, in time, destroy this state and nation unless we act to stop it.

Brown is also a dedicated advocate of the government condemning private property for "public use," whatever that may be. This means homes and businesses are taken from rightful owners and turned over to developers for a more publicly beneficial use. As Oakland's Mayor, Brown presided over the use of condemnation to acquire long-term family businesses which were in turn passed on to political cronies, in the guise of "developers."

When all things are considered, Gov. Moonbeam was then, and is now, nothing more than the committed leftist of which we should by now, have had enough of. Brown is a bundle of known and fatally flawed goods. He is a consummate politician controlled and driven by countless biases and hidden agendas. At first, these were hard to detect, as in his first term as Governor. Now we know for certain they exist. We now have no excuse for being surprised by his intent to impose these agendas again if he becomes our chief executive in November 2010.

During those eight years as Governor, Brown largely imposed his biases and pursued his agenda(s) with impunity. Notably, he did so when he used his power to appoint judges, the heads of law enforcement, parole, and regulatory agencies. He did so in deliberately provocative ways. He often chose loose cannons and radicals to run the state's most important agencies. He apparently reveled in the discord and division he inflicted on the state government and the people of California. Like Obama, he promised to be different, better, a harbinger of hope and change. Nothing truly is new under the sun. Voters believed him and were grievously wrong to do so. They would be grievously wrong to do so again.

The main life-and-death reason not to re-anoint him is that the Moonbeam will almost certainly resume his agenda with the courts. That was, and remains, the most destructive aspect of his administration, and the one with the most far-reaching effects. It is very difficult to remedy gubernatorial appointments in the administrative realm, and almost, but not quite, impossible to do so in the judicial realm. This book illustrates why and demonstrates that we, as voters, hold our fate in our own hands concerning his election. He must be rejected for the high office of Governor and we must deprive him of the chance to ever appoint anyone to anything of consequence in government.

This is a vital matter. The nation is in grave circumstances because of the biases and hidden agendas of Obama and the Progressives. The situation in California is equally grave, if not more so, and will only be exacerbated if Brown is returned to power.

There is a specific, personal reason to reject Jerry Brown this time. Since his tenure as Governor, and despite his awful legacy, California actually has come a long way in fostering public safety, providing rights to crime victims, and ensuring guilty criminals, especially the violent ones are punished. It was not easy, as you will see. It took years after Brown was out of office to finally accomplish this. Giving him the green light now, puts all this effort at risk.

Even now, there are still errors in the administration of criminal justice. Some of the errors are institutional. Some are attributable to human error, but on careful investigation, even these can be considered to be institutional because they involve a lack of training, oversight, or involve an excessive deference to the leadership of government worker labor unions.

A distinction should be drawn between errors and the biases and hidden agendas discussed. Errors do occur and must be rectified as soon as possible, particularly when they deleteriously impact public safety. Biases and hidden agendas are more insidious, and far from obvious. They work and spread in obscured and injurious ways. They are subtle poisons. As such, they are difficult to diagnose and remedy, particularly when they come from an executive, like a Gov. Moonbeam, who has the power to appoint the heads of law enforcement and parole agencies.

Worst of all, biases and hidden agendas are the most difficult to diagnose and remedy when they belong to an executive, like a Gov. Moonbeam, who has the power to appoint judges at all court levels: the trial courts, the appellate courts, and the state Supreme Court. When Brown appointed three biased justices with hidden agendas to the California Supreme Court, especially Rose Bird, a former public defender and Brown's chauffeur (yes, she was Brown's driver), it took the people of this state almost a decade to fully diagnose and remedy the situation by the extremely rare event of voting these judges out of office. Does anyone believe Brown will not actively begin to re-establish an activist, left-wing judicial axis, or that he will not act in concert with the identical appointment philosophy of Barack Obama? We must not allow that to happen.

Because of Brown's unwillingness to recognize and protect the rights of crime victims and, more generally, to promote public safety during his terms as Governor, the people had to begin protecting themselves. This led directly to the landmark Proposition 8. Prop 8 was the beginning of a decades-long process of self-help by voters that is still underway. Other criminal justice initiatives were adopted by voters only after again concluding the administration of criminal justice, specifically, and the government generally, were not being responsive. These efforts include: Prop 115, the Crime Victims' Justice Reform Act of 1990; Prop 184, the Three Strikes Initiative in 1994; Prop 21, the Juvenile Justice Initiative in 2000; and, Prop 209, the Crime Victims' Bill of Rights Act in 2008, or Marsy's Law. All of these came about in reaction to the Brown-era abuses. Now is not time to turn back the clock. Now is not the time to batter down the relatively secure bastion of public safety we've manage to re-erect for ourselves.

All we have to do as California Voters this time is to review the record and reflect on what Jerry Brown did in his previous tenure to get a picture of what he will certainly do again if given the chance. Should we be so heedless, or so negligent, or indeed, so reckless to put him back in the state's highest office? If so, and the same or similar calamities ensue, we will have only ourselves to blame. To avoid this grievous mistake, the same grievous mistake made in electing Obama to the nation's highest office two years ago, all we have to do is say, "No, we won't!

Ever so often we get the chance to get it right, to undo a mistake or to keep from repeating it. Voting down Jerry Brown is that chance. Pray, citizens and voters, and get it right.

CHAPTER TWENTY ONE

JUDICIAL ACTIVISM: GOVERNMENT BY DECREE

By L. Thaxton Hanson
Associate Justice, Court of Appeal
State of California

The concept of a democratic form of government is of ancient origin. The word democracy stems from the Greek word "democratia" which means rule of the people. The Athenian orator-statesman Pericles in his historic "Funeral Address" at the public burial of men who had died fighting the Spartans (430 B.C.) said: "Our Constitution is named a democracy, because it is in the hands not of the few but of the many."

The dilemma of how to make the judicial branch accountable to the citizens under our tripartite form of constitutional government has plagued our nation since its inception. In the early days, the debate primarily revolved around the divergent philosophical views held by Alexander Hamilton and the Federalists on the one hand, and those of the Thomas Jefferson and the Republicans on the other.

The autocratic Hamiltonians not only wanted a strong central government, but advocated long or life terms for appointed judges on the federal and state levels.

The Jeffersonians wanted decentralized government and short tenure for judges, with easy removal from the bench. Jefferson had definite reservations about the prerogatives of judges. These reservations were not because he perceived judges to be venal, but because he knew them to be human. The one salient thought that permeates all of Jefferson's writings is: "Trust the People."

In today's debate on how to make California's judicial branch more responsive and accountable to the people, the contestants are not usually referred to as Jeffersonians and

Hamiltonians, but are characterized as "strict construction-ists" and "judicial activists."

The strict constructionists endorse the traditional doctrine of "judicial restraint" and view their role primarily as one of interpreting rather than making law. They recognize that activism in respect to far-reaching social change should come from the political (elected) branches of government — the legislative and executive.

Judges who exercise judicial restraint display a keen awareness of the basic constitutional concept of separation of powers. They are aware that no one branch of government is supreme over the others, but that all three are co-equal with checks and balances.

Originally, the judicial function was to resolve disputes. But in 1803, in Marbury v. Madison judicial power was expanded to include "judicial review" — the authority to rule on whether the actions of the other branches conform to constitutional prescriptions. Even with the awesome authority to nullify legislative enactments, the courts were able for many years to command a high degree of public confidence due to self-imposed restraint from making incursions into the legislative domain.

Strict constructionists have no quarrel with the doctrine of judicial review, but assert that restraint should be used — the power should be sparingly employed.

While the present United States Supreme Court has been using restraint and displaying a pronounced deference to the elected branches of government, the same has not been true of California's Supreme Court, which (under Chief Justice Rose Bird) is dominated by judicial activists.

Michael A. Musmanno, former Justice of the Pennsylvania Supreme Court and Presiding Judge at the Nuremberg Trials, has pointed out that when judicial activists "sit as a super-legislature", they are guilty of usurpation of power "which, in itself, is unconstitutional."

Among the activists on the California Supreme Court has been the late Mathew O. Tobriner. In an article entitled "Can Young Lawyers Reform Society Through the Courts?", published several years ago in the California State Bar Journal, Tobriner said: "courts are capable of creative judicial response to pressures for readjustment of societal relationships, and that reform of society need not be confined to legislative halls in the near future there will be, if anything,

119

an increasing need that the demands for social reform - and even for social 'revolution' — be pressed in the judicial sphere and framed in the context of legal relationships .... Young lawyers will probe, question and challenge the legal rules and the mores of the day ... they will press for the acceptance of new social values."

Justice Tobriner presents us with the spectacle of a high court judge exhorting and inviting social engineers with law degrees, representing liberal special interest groups bent on imposing their own social ideology to file their lawsuits which "activist" judges can then smugly assert they are "compelled" to and "must" decide. In this manner, by flagrantly usurping the legislative function, judicial activists can ram through societal changes which reflect their personal social theory by means of judicial decree.

In this way a minority can short-circuit the constitutionally established political process and unconstitutionally force their will on the majority. Is this democracy? And does it not establish an extremely dangerous concept in motion which could ultimately destroy a free society?

The judicial activists on the California Supreme Court have been wielding arbitrary power like a battle ax. They have arrogantly cut deep into every facet of California society in their efforts to reshape it into a society fashioned after their personal visions of what "ought to be."

A prominent Ventura County lawyer once wrote Governor Edmund G. (Jerry) Brown that "(In) civil law, the (State Supreme) court has recently introduced uncertainty where there was certainty, favored unethical and irresponsible citizens over the ethical and responsible citizen, assured the future filing of many cases and appeals which formerly were considered without foundation, and introduced judicial legislation in place of constitutional statutory law enacted by the Legislature."

In the criminal law field, the adverse effects of judicial activism are glaring and catastrophic. A primary purpose of every government is to maintain an orderly society by providing security for its citizens against attack by criminally-minded predators. California citizens pay very high taxes for the government to provide such security. But while criminals roam the streets, the citizens have become prisoners in their own homes and as a matter of self-preservation have collectively expended additional millions turning their homes into fortresses by installing iron bars on their windows and burglar alarms, and by arming themselves with handguns and Mace.

Unquestionably the enormous loss of public confidence in California's criminal justice system is due to the general perception that the law, as administered by the activists in our State Supreme Court, is grossly out of balance and favors the criminals over the victims.

A classic example of judicial activism run amuck is the manner in which the California Supreme Court has continuously ignored the collective wisdom and will of the people in regards to the death penalty. This arrogance has created a massive loss of public confidence in the criminal justice system. In 1972 the Court, in the Anderson decision, declared the long standing death penalty statute unconstitutional as cruel and unusual punishment. In so doing, they freed 111 felons from death row, and made them eligible for parole.

By mid-1980 about 60 more capital punishment cases had built up in the California Supreme Court. Of the ten cases decided as of this writing, eight were reversed for one reason or another. Only two death penalty cases were affirmed on a split vote — and those surely will continue to face protracted judicial review.

Judicial activism is completely at odds with the basic constitutional principle of separation of powers. The United States Constitution begins with the words "We the people." Lincoln, in his Gettysburg Address, described our's as a government "of the people, by the people, and for the people." When these basic American concepts are flagrantly breached by judicial activists, who are not answerable to the people, frustration mounts and public confidence in our system of government plummets.

Although the lower courts must accept as binding authority the decisions rendered by the activists on our highest court, the court of public opinion is not similarly bound.

California's system of justice is fundamentally sound. However, like a highly prized Stradivarius violin out of tune, it needs retuning to correct the discordant notes struck by the judicial activists. The basic constitutional question is: Under our form of government, whose just powers are supposed to be derived from the consent of the governed, should a small clique of appointed judicial activists have unbridled power and be accountable to no one but themselves?

Fortunately, under California's constitutional form of representative government, the State Supreme Court is not "the Court of Last Resort." The Court of Last Resort, ultimately, is still the collective will of the people expressed through the ballot box. While the activists may continue to ignore that will and drag their feet on implementing the public mandate, they cannot and dare not react in the same fashion to a constitutional amendment placing into effect measures making the courts more accountable to the public.

In the words of Thomas Jefferson: "Trust the People."

CHAPTER TWENTY TWO

JUDICIAL TYRANNY
AN INJUSTICE TO THE CONSTITUTION
AND PUBLIC

By Clyde Small

(Clyde Small served five years on the Shasta County Superior Court. He resigned in August, 1979. He previously served as a foreign service officer for the State Department.)

For the past 25 years (written when Bird was Chief Justice), government power has shifted steadily toward the courts. This has not been by a decision of the voters to change the structure of government. Neither is it due to any overt "open and notorious" claim by the courts that their original and traditional constitutional powers should be expanded.

Because courts govern by deciding specific cases, re-action to decisions is usually confined to those directly involved. Whether by accident or design, few individual decisions have increased court powers to proportions which would produce direct confrontations with the other branches of government or with the public. The gradual increase in court powers has produced comment and debate which is miniscule compared to what would certainly have followed if such a change in the division of power had been proposed as a formal constitutional amendment.

Recently, however, the number of people and interests alienated by the growing powers of the courts has begun to reach a critical mass. The increase in debate about the courts make it possible to objectively study whether the changes are wise or feasible when measured by political science and the axioms of our culture. We may, and must, look at policy making by the judiciary in terms of how well it works in solving problems, in comparison to other methods. And we must examine what side effects such judicial activities have upon other institutions, with special emphasis on the administration of justice itself.

In contrast to many others which "just growed", the design of government in the United States was engineered by the framers of the federal constitution. Guided by a mature understanding of history, they produced a brilliant plan which has been generally copied in the several states, and even in many other nations.

The fundamental concept in that design is separation and balance of government power. Power was divided among the legislature, the executive, and the judiciary in such a manner that the power of each could be exercised separately, but that each would act as a check and balance against the others. The dynamic symmetry of the resulting structure has withstood the turbulence of almost two centuries of unprecedented change in the size of the area governed, and in human condition, without significant deformity.

Under the founding fathers' plan, the legislature was to crystallize public policy into written laws. The executive was to turn those laws into action. The function of the Supreme Court, as originally defined, was merely to decide individual cases in controversy. An important vacuum in the system was filled early by the Supreme Court's assumption, of the power of judicial review. It became the arbiter of whether the other branches were acting constitutionally.

Napoleon said that a constitution should be brief and ambiguous. The framers of the United States Constitution thought otherwise. They believed a constitution should provide stability. Ambiguity and facile provisions for amendment confers no stability. The amendment process in our Constitution is deliberately cumbersome in order to discourage impetuous change.

The judiciary, in order to decide cases, had to fill gaps in the Constitution as well as in acts of Congress. For 150 years they did so by consulting the intent of the framers. The courts developed the self-imposed doctrine of judicial restraint. With this approach, the nation avoided the hazards which would follow from the executive and legislature being free to define their own authority. No similar device was developed to prevent the courts from doing the same because nobody expected this to be a problem. The courts were neither intended nor generally disposed to legislate, and their conduct over hundreds of years before the adoption of the federal Constitution had earned them a high level of public trust and respect.

A related, but separate policy was continued in the form developed by the English courts as stare decisis. The Supreme Court considered itself free to decide questions of constitutional interpretation. But once such an issue was decided, the Court was reluctant to change its mind. This policy gives the lower courts (and the public) the assurance of stability in law. Stare decisis also encourages more careful decisions by the Supreme Court itself. Reversal of a rule or decision is still possible, but it must be accomplished by compelling argument, and by the court which made the rule or decision in question.

Until the late 1930's, the United States Supreme Court generally adhered to the tradition. Its noteworthy vice at the end of that time was not a tendency to enact law, but to carry to extremes its power to strike down acts of Congress as "unconstitutional." During the same period, however, the country moved rapidly towards big government. The resulting problems were intensified by World War II and the international role acquired by the United States afterwards. The Supreme Court began to relieve pressures upon Congress by itself issuing decisions which were the equivalent of innovative legislation.

By varying degrees of choice, state courts fell into line with the new judicial activism. But in the past decade the U.S. Supreme Court has begun to noticeably recede from this intensified activist role. But the California State Supreme Court has gone in the other direction - towards even greater activism. We see, for example, statements in California decisions that criminals in this state are entitled to more protection of rights and immunities than those guaranteed by the greatly liberalized federal Constitution.

Until around 1960, the courts of last resort clothed their innovations with the pretense of "interpretation." Ingenious distinctions and scholarly footnotes paid lip service to stare decisis, but there was scarcely an advance sheet which did not contain at least one drastic change in law. Then, well after litigants and attorneys had begun protesting that the courts were in fact legislating, the courts began to frankly admit it. Once the courts had, with apparent safety, completed the transition into a legislature, they could begin including effective dates, and urgency clauses into their decisions.

All of this, having been gradually accomplished, never precipitated any pitched battle with either the public of the other branches of government. Actually, the federal and state legislatures may have been relieved to have some of the hottest political grounders fielded by appellate judges who were insulated from political repercussions. Many of the judicial enactments have been popular, at least with influential interest groups. Some of those decisions have been wise and beneficial. But none of these circumstances necessarily means that the change in the structure of government power is desirable. To make that determination requires a look at other things.

Courts of the last resort (the federal and various state supreme courts) probably have, on the average, members who are better educated and more intelligent than do legislatures. The minimum standards of entry, although sometimes evaded, are usually more exacting on the courts than on the legislatures. The procedures in the courts are more rigorous, and the quality of preparation is normally higher. By contrast, those appearing before legislative committees often wind up completely confused, and there is seldom a pretense of making an orderly, point-by-point evaluation of conflicting contentions.

The extensive time which legislators must spend in running for office distracts resources which might be applied to solving the enormous problems before him. Judges are free from this distraction.

Judges have not needed to explain their decisions to those adversely affected. Anyone who presses too hard for that relief may find himself summarily in custody for contempt of court. This removes an inhibition which is present at all levels for legislators. It would be political suicide for a legislator to impose such a sanction, even if he had the power to do so.

Finally, courts are much more compact bodies for making decisions, and can almost always reach one, whereas legislatures can become paralyzed by political pressures and their own cumbersome internal procedures.

Taken together, the foregoing are good arguments for the virtue of government by the small elite in an undemocratic society - in political science terminology, by an oligarchy.

What drawbacks, then, must be weighed against those

advantages? There are many, and of a magnitude which should attract a good deal more attention from political scientists and legal scholars — as well as from the other branches of government and from the public, and even the long suffering lower courts and attorneys.

Legislation by the courts in the areas of substantive law is without legitimacy. It is a usurpation of power and function, and is hardly made less so because it was surreptitious. Judges are, after all, as much fiduciaries to the public as any other public officer. They ought to be even more scrupulous in assuring that the power they exercise has been freely, regularly, and formally granted.

It is argued that the legislatures are no longer equal to their responsibilities, and the courts are merely filling a vacuum which the public interest demands. There is some truth to this. But if government by the judiciary is the answer, why not give the public a straightforward presentation of the idea on which the courts are fond of calling the "marketplace of ideas" — and allow that "truth" to gain acceptance?

The courts are not, by nature, equipped to respond to the will of the majority. If one really believes in democratic principles, that is a fatal vice. Often the courts are not really as concerned with majority opinion as in protection of the rights of the minority. Those rights need protection, but in extremes exaltation of minorities may be even less wholesome than discrimination in favor of the majority. Classic democratic theory is that any power the court has is based upon the consent of the majority.

But supreme court judges do not work in an environment which thrusts them into contact with the grass roots. They are neither paid to sample public opinion nor given any staff or machinery to do so. They meet individual litigants themselves only through court records, and these individuals often fall short of being representative of all those who will be affected by a decision. The court does have access to the media, to law review articles, and to unofficial social contacts. But they would recoil at being told a trial judge based a decision upon that kind of evidence.

It is much the same with the facts of a case. The supreme court judges do not have the trial judge's power to call witnesses, subpoena documents, or view premises. They are bound by the discretion of trial record. The record is often misleading even in the trial court, and does

127

not approach the quality of the record of a good legislative committee as a foundation for legislation. Much of what a legislator would demand to know cannot even be ethically included in an appellate brief. Further limitations are imposed by the competence and loyalties of counsel — what is good for the public may not be good for any particular litigants before the court.

The courts, then, see a subject through a very narrow, clouded viewpoint. It is virtually impossible to frame a judicial decision which sensitively, knowledgeably and comprehensively regulates an activity in the same manner as good chapter law.

When a supreme court initiates sweeping changes in substance law, it does so with a "leading decision" followed by gradual clarifications over a period of many years. The trial courts and lawyers are left in suspense and uncertainty, which is aggravated by numerous decisions related to the issue but which have little congruency. Before full clarification occurs, a new leading case often regenerates the whole noxious process.

The clarification process is delayed by the fact that the supreme courts have no power generally to issue supplementary regulations or bulletins on their own motion. They must wait for the right case to be brought up by litigants to resolve dangling questions. This takes time and contributes heavily to the multiplicity of suits and delays in justice.

Since the supreme courts' primary area of legislation has been in the form of de facto amendments to the constitutions themselves, the vice is compounded. Such decisions cannot be corrected by anyone else if they cause mischief or are unpopular. The courts have no reliable means of correcting their own mistakes by following them with supervision. A decision which has catastrophic impact upon trial courts or the public is not open to correction by a supreme court on its own motion even if it has some means of learning about the problem.

This reaches a point of absurdity in criminal prosecutions. Because the state has no appeal from an acquittal, and because the trial judge must apply the law as stated by the supreme court, the prosecutor often has no way of bringing cases up which show the inappropriate results of the rule when practically applied. So far as the supreme court is concerned, the problem has been solved by its decision.

But in reality the trial process has been deformed in favor of the defendant. If experience under the decision brands it a failure, the supreme court can truly say that is has officially heard nothing of the problem.

One of the worst consequences of activist supreme courts is the multiplication of suits and the expansion of delays and uncertainty. Once it is known that a supreme court is disposed to make changes, many appeals are taken even when a trial was in exact conformity with the rules then existing. These appeals, which would be frivolous in a healthy system, have been vindicated so often that a criminal defense attorney is probably guilty of malpractice if he does not appeal every case. Trial judges are also made preoccupied with a fear of reversal and begin to anticipate further liberalized changes, thus making prosecution of criminals even more difficult.

Reversals also generate more trials. The uncertainty of the rules of proceedings leads many guilty defendants to elect for a trial on the hope that someone will forget something - and he will be freed on a legal technicality.

The increased work-load of the courts has produced haste, uncertainty, fatigue, and near desperation at the trial court level. Though the supreme courts seem complacent about it, delay and uncertainty in the administration of justice are probably worse evils than any the supreme courts have undertaken to correct by their adventures into public policy. The trend is towards limitless review and reexamination of the issues -reflecting the inability to believe that something has been done right and should be laid to rest. An individual who showed these symptoms would be diagnosed as an anxiety case.

The civil litigant, who pays for the whole mess, has been wedged out of the legal system in many areas because criminal cases are entitled to precedence. At best his case is delayed, and it may get insufficient attention from a court which is at the end of its resources.

The criminal defendant is better off, but not entirely so. In court he is generally baffled, and often incredulous, at the complexity and byzantine subtlety of the proceedings. The ponderous ritual which is believed to protect him from a ruthless public in fact puts him to sleep, and he responds appropriately only at a nudge from his lawyer. The whole proceeding is becoming a dehumanized caricature, and criminals generally regard it with little respect.

The end product of it all is that antisocial elements are encouraged, defended, and nurtured to an ever increasing extent. And crime has increased. If the trend continues, one wonders why the supreme courts are not willing to leave the work to someone else.

All of this has eroded public respect for the courts and for the administration of justice. Public attitude towards the courts, once bordering on veneration, now oscillates between suspicion and contempt. That attitude would only be intensified if the condition of affairs were better known and understood.

In assuming prerogatives of the legislative branch of government, the courts have taken on a responsibility they are not equipped to discharge well. While officiously occupying themselves with the work of another branch of government, they have badly neglected their own. They have overloaded the entire judicial system, undermined the reputation of the courts, and impaired the morale of the legal system.

It is unlikely that Americans want to be ruled by an oligarchy, judicial or otherwise, no matter how elite and idealistic its membership. Continuing to attempt to impose one by the judiciary may well comprise the ability of the courts to discharge their proper function — which it can do with distinction if it concentrates on it.

The whole adventure into policy-making has turned out badly, and should be abandoned before things get worse.

CHAPTER TWENTY THREE

HOW COURT DECISIONS AND PRACTICES HAMPER PROSECUTION

By
Edwin Meese III
Former United States Attorney General

The late William James
Former Senior Assistant Attorney General
State or California

The right of personal security is natural right which is inherent and inalienable.

Appellate Court Justice Norman Elkington explained that right in an opinion by saying "the safety of the people from criminal and other aggression was (and is) guarded by the 'highest law.' Inherent in this pledge was (and is) the right of the people to governmental protection from crime and violence."

Appellate Justice Macklin Fleming, in his book The Price of Perfect Justice, stated that: "Written law now is routinely qualified, rewritten or repealed by the courts acting under the authority of natural law, fundamental law, or divine revelation." It is not surprising that scholars all over America have, during the past few years, taken an active roll in questioning "government by judiciary."

As "government by judiciary" has rapidly grown, a discernible decline in legislative authority has been the result. According to Fleming: "With this decline of legislative authority, a certain reversal of function between legislature and courts has taken place. Instead of the legislature instructing the courts on the general rules of law that the courts should follow in deciding particular cases, the courts have been instructing the legislature on what laws the legislature can adopt and how those laws should be written. As a consequence of such judicial expansionism, in many fields of law the legislature merely echoes legislative acts that have been initially enacted into law by the courts."

This, says Fleming, has permitted the U.S. Supreme Court "to acquire the absolute power to decide any case or controversy arising within the United States, absolute power to invalidate any act of the President or of Congress and absolute power to control virtually all acts of state government, whether legislative, executive, or judicial."

Justices themselves have agreed. "We are under a Constitution, but the Constitution is what the judges say it is ..." wrote Charles Evans Hughes. "... The only check upon our exercise of power is our sense of self-restraint," said Harlan Stone. "As the decisions now stand, I see hardly any limit but the sky to invalidating of those rights if they happen to strike a majority of this court as for any reason undesirable," commented Oliver Wendel Holmes. Similar statements have been made by Justices Robert H. Jackson, Felix Frankfurter, Hugo Black, John M. Harlan, and others.

Most of the justices made their remarks in dissenting opinions. That is to be expected, according to Fleming, because justices deplore absolute judicial power only when they find themselves in the minority — on a particular issue. "Yet this circumstance in no way undermines the validity of their comments," declares Fleming, "nor does it impair the accuracy of their observations on the exercise of absolute judicial power, a power which in practical operation establishes the personal views and convictions of a majority of the members of the U.S. Supreme Court as the supreme law of the land."

The phrase, "the irrelevance of guilt," is one used by Lord Diplock of the British House of Lords in referring to the American rules of criminal law that require suppression of all evidence obtained by unlawful, improper, or irregular means. "The American rule on the subject of illegally obtained evidence," says Fleming, "has flip-flopped from one that suppresses no evidence to one that suppresses all illegally obtained evidence, and throughout its use in this country the rule has been generally applied in an all-or-nothing fashion. Prior to 1914, American jurisprudence took the view that evidence relevant to the issue before the tribunal was admissible evidence regardless of its source and regardless of the means by which it had been brought before the tribunal."

The federal courts, in 1914, adopted a policy prohibiting use in federal prosecutions of evidence that had been illegally obtained by federal officers. The California Supreme Court in 1955 adopted a policy prohibiting the use in California courts of illegally obtained evidence. The assumption behind these policies was that the incentive of officers to break the law would largely disappear if the illegally obtained evidence could not be used in court. These earlier rulings were primarily based on court policy, and as such they could be modified if they did not work out. But in 1961 the United States Supreme Court ruled, as a matter of constitutional law, that illegally obtained evidence could not be admitted in any state criminal prosecution.

In many instances, the rules for suppression of evidence have become so complicated and their nuances so subtle that judges of the highest courts, years after the event, divide among themselves, five to four, or four to three, on the legality of a particular search or interrogation.

A technical and mechanical interpretation of the requirements for the suppression of illegally obtained evidence purports to reduce to computer formula the legality of investigative efforts used by law enforcement officers to solve a crime, and leads to bizarre results. This is particularly true when a judicial decision changes the rules, as periodically happens, and applies those changes retroactively. Thus, what was legal when the police conducted a particular search, can be declared "illegal" by a judicial decision rendered years later. What deterrence of alleged police misconduct is that? Such absurd results only breed contempt for the courts.

English courts evaluate the problem of suppression of evidence as one of striking a balance between the individual's interest in freedom from intrusion and society's interest in maintaining order and suppression of crime. Purely technical violations do not foreclose the use of improperly obtained evidence. Thus, there exists in the English system a flexibility wholly lacking in the American system. That lack of flexibility has come under increasing attacks — and properly so.

Unfortunately, California's appellate courts demonstrated a continuing trend to exclude relevant and probative evidence which would be otherwise admissible in court in the truth-finding process. Society has a vital interest in the criminal process that assures that those guilty of crime be brought to book and that law-abiding citizens are guaranteed life, liberty, and the pursuit of happiness. Those accused of crime have their rights to a fair trial in accordance with the Bill of Rights. Our judicial process, just as in the English system, should require there be a balancing of these sometimes competing interests. An extravagant statement, at one extreme, is that it is better to let a hundred guilty men go free than for one innocent man to be convicted. Obviously, no one wants an innocent man convicted, but to assure this, must 100 guilty men be freed to again prey on peaceful citizens? Let's hope that the odds against society are not that great!

Roscoe Pound recognized the dangers of such a system when he declared, "(Our legal tradition) is so zealous to secure fair play to the individual that often it secures very little fair play to the public." The increase in crime, particularly violent crime, has caused concern that there is an imbalance against society in the continued exclusion of relevant evidence during the judicial process.

One of the most promising recent developments in criminal justice has been an increased attention to the rights of victims. For too many years it appeared that government had lost sight of its primary reason for existence - to protect its citizen's life, liberty, and property against those who would harm them. Finally, public officials, community organizations, and criminal justice agencies have re-discovered that the victim is an essential party to the criminal justice process.

The need to recognize and protect the rights of the victim was aptly described more than 40 (now 70) years ago by Justice Cardozo who said, "The concept of fairness must not be strained till it is narrowed to a filament. We are to keep the balance true." Society has a long way to go before that balance is restored, but at least progress is being made.

The time has come to ask hard questions and seek responsible answers to the dilemma posed to our democratic society by "government by judiciary," and by the practice of the "irrelevance of guilt," and for answers remembering the victims of crime. It won't do for the Legislature to defer to the courts. It won't do for the courts to remain in the undemocratic shadows of "judicial independence" which serves not to protect the integrity of the courts, but to promote judicial arrogance and loss of public confidence in the fairness and effectiveness of the courts.

The courts, to paraphrase Justice Jackson, are not final because they are infallible, but they are infallible only because they are final.

Edwin Meese III is a former Attorney General to President Ronald Reagan. He is a former director of the Center for Criminal Justice Policy and Management and adjunct professor of law at the University of San Diego School of Law. Meese served as Legal Affairs Advisor to California Governor Ronald Reagan. He has served as the Ronald Reagan Distinguished Fellow in Public Policy and Chairman of the Center for Legal and Judicial Studies at the Heritage Foundation.

The late William E. James was a Senior Assistant Attorney General of California and served in the Attorney General's Office from 1947 until his death.

FOOTNOTES

Chapter One — The High Court

1. *Los Angeles Herald Examiner*, October 21, 1979,
   San Francisco Chronicle, October 20, 1979
2. *Los Angeles Herald Examiner*, October 21, 1979,
   San Francisco Chronicle, October 20, 1979
3. *Fresno Bee*, September 21, 1979
   Chronicle 4. Offense and Service Report; Case C74—07593
   Office of the Sheriff, County of Marin, California
5. Inter-Departmental Communication; California Prison at San Quentin;
   Statement of Correctional Officer L. B. Bledseo, 18 July, 1974
6. *San Francisco Examiner*, May 27, 1978
7. *Los Angeles Herald Examiner*, October 21, 1979
8. *San Francisco Examiner*, May 21, 1978
   Sacramento Union, May 21, 1978
9. *Los Angeles Times*, October 10, 1979
10. *Fresno Bee* (UPI), October 20, 1979
    San Francisco, October 24, 1979
11. *San Francisco Chronicle*, October 24, 1979
12. *San Francisco Chronicle*, October 24, 1979
13. *San Francisco Chronicle*, October 24, 1979
14. *San Francisco Chronicle*, September 20, 1979

Chapter Two — What Are Friends For Anyway?

1. *Los Angeles Times*, February 13, 1980
2. *Sacramento Union*, April 20, 1978
3. *Los Angeles Times*, January 15, 1977
4. *Sacramento Union*, March 30, 1978
5. *Los Angeles Times*, February 13, 1980
6. *Los Angeles Times*, February 13, 1980
7. *Los Angeles Herald Examiner*, March 9, 1980
8. *Los Angeles Herald Examiner*, March 9, 1980
9. *Los Angeles Herald Examiner*, March 9, 1980
10. *Los Angeles Herald Examiner*, March 9, 1980
11. *Los Angeles Herald Examiner*, March 9, 1980
12. *Los Angeles Herald Examiner*, March 9, 1980
13. Records of the Sonoma County District Attorney's Office, dated
    October 10, 1978; December 15, 1978; December 4, 1979
14. *Los Angeles Herald Examiner*, March 9, 1980
15. *Los Angeles Herald Examiner*, March 9, 1980
    Santa Rosa Press Democrat, January 30, 1980
16. *Los Angeles Herald Examiner*, March 9, 1980
    Santa Rosa Press Democrat, January 30, 1980
17. *Los Angeles Herald Examiner*, March 9, 1980
18. *Los Angeles Herald Examiner*, March 9, 1980
19. *Los Angeles Herald Examiner*, March 9, 1980
20. *Los Angeles Herald Examiner*, March 9, 1980
21. *Los Angeles Herald Examiner*, March 9, 1980
22. *Human Events*, Capital Briefs, March 27, 1982
23. *Santa Rosa Press Democrat*, February 3, 1980
24. *Santa Rosa Press Democrat*, February 3, 1980

25. *Los Angeles Times*, February 13, 1980
26. *Santa Rosa Press Democrat*, February 3, 1980
27. *Los Angeles Times*, February 13, 1980
    Santa Rosa Press Democrat, February 3, 1980
28. *Santa Rosa Press Democrat*, February 3, 1980
29. *Los Angeles Times*, February 13, 1980
30. *Los Angeles Times*, February 13, 1980
31. *Los Angeles Times*, February 13, 1980
32. *Los Angeles Times*, February 13, 1980
33. *Sacramento Union*, January 16, 1980
34. California Fair Political Practices Commission, Campaign Contribution
    and Spending Reports, June 1978 page B-2; November 1978 Pages B-39 &
    B-51
35. *Independent Press-Telegram*, January 17, 1980
36. *Los Angeles Herald Examiner*, February 15, 1980
37. *Sacramento Union*, January 16, 1980
38. *Independent Press-Telegram*, January 17, 1980
39. *Independent Press-Telegram*, January 17, 1980
40. *Independent Press-Telegram*, January 17, 1980
41. *Independent Press-Telegram*, January 17, 1980
42. *Los Angeles Herald Examiner*, January 15, 1980
43. *Independent Press-Telegram*, January 17, 1980
44. *Santa Rosa Press Democrat*, January 30, 1980
45. *Los Angeles Herald Examiner*, September 20, 1980
46. *Los Angeles Times*, March 12, 1982

Chapter Three — More Friends

1. *Pasadena Star News*, January 12, 1982
2. *Courts and Judges*,
3. *Star News*, January 28, 1982
4. District Attorney's "Motion For Disqualification of a Judge", People
   v. Gabourie, et al, January 11, 1982, Los Angeles County Superior
   Court
5. Judge Alston's "Answer of Judge to Motion For Disqualification," case
   cited in note 4
6. *Star News*, January 28, 1982
7. *Star News*, July 22, 1977
8. *Star News*, July 22, 1977
9. *Star News*, July 22, 1977
10. *Star News*, July 22, 1977
11. *Star News*, July 22, 1977
12. *Star News*, July 22, 1977
13. *Star News*, July 22, 1977
14. *Star News*, July 22, 1977
15. *Star News*, July 22, 1977
16. *Star News*, July 22, 1977
17. *Star News*, July 22, 1977
18. *Star News*, July 22, 1977
19. Memorandum To: David R. Disco, Head Deputy, Pasadena Branch, Los
    Angeles District Attorney's Office; From: Brent Riggs, Calendar
    Deputy, Department H; Subject: People v. Debby Sue Vanella, Case A
    587803; Dated: March 16, 1981
20. Letter from Burbank Chief of Police James L. Shaffer to the
    Commission on Judicial Performance, dated April 9. 1981
21. See Memorandum, note 18

22. See Memorandum, note 18 and Letter, note 19
23. See Memorandum, note 18
24. See Memorandum, note 18
25. See Memorandum, note 18
26. See Memorandum, note 18
27. See Letter, note 19
28. See Letter, note 19
29. Letter from Los Angeles Supervisor Mike Antonovich to the Commission on Judicial Performance, dated May 15, 1981.
30. Letter from Jack Frankel to Chief of Police James Shaffer, dated June 17, 1981.
31. *Star News*, August 30, 1981
32. *Star News*, August 30, 1981
33. *Star News*, August 21, 1981
34. *Los Angeles Metropolitan News*, March 15, 1982
35. *Los Angeles Metropolitan News*, March 15, 1982
36. *Los Angeles Times*, June 5, 1982

Chapter Four — Contempt of Court

1. *Los Angeles Daily News*, December 2, 1981, p. 20
2. *Los Angeles Daily News*, September 24, 1981
3. *Los Angeles Daily News*, September 24, 1981
4. *Los Angeles Daily News*, September 24, 1981
5. *Los Angeles Daily News*, December 2, 1981
6. Testimony by the Citizens for Law and Order to the Commission on Judicial Appointments, December 26, 1978.
7. *Oakland Tribune*, November 10, 1978
8. *Oakland Tribune*, November 21, 1978
9. *Oakland Tribune*, February 22, 1980
10. *Oakland Tribune*, July 10, 1980
11. *Oakland Tribune*, July 10, 1980
12. *Oakland Tribune*, February 23, 1980
13. *Oakland Tribune*, February 22, 1980
14. *Oakland Tribune*, February 22, 1980
15. *Oakland Tribune*, July 12, 1980
16. *Oakland Tribune*, February 23, 1980
17. *Oakland Tribune*, February 23, 1980
18. *Oakland Tribune*, July 12, 1980
19. *Oakland Tribune*, July 12, 1980

Chapter Five — The Law and the Prophet

1. *Fresno Bee*, February 5, 1976
2. *Fresno Bee*, April 3, 1977
   Fresno Bee, May 29, 1978
3. *Fresno Bee*, May 24, 1977
   Fresno Bee, June 17, 1978
4. *Fresno Bee*, May 24, 1977
5. *Fresno Bee*, June 17, 1978
6. *Fresno Bee*, July 16, 1978
7. *Fresno Bee*, May 21, 1977
8. *Fresno Bee*, June 17, 1978
9. *Fresno Bee*, June 9, 1977
10. *Fresno Bee*, May 24, 1977
11. *Fresno Bee*, June 17, 1978

12. *Fresno Bee*, June 30, 1978
13. *Fresno Bee*, February 4, 1978
14. *Fresno Bee*, June 7, 1978

Chapter Six — The Gangs All Here

1. *Fresno Bee*, July 11, 1981
2. *Fresno Bee*, July 11, 1981
3. *Fresno Bee*, July 11, 1981
4. *Los Angeles Times*, November 4, 1978
5. *Los Angeles Times*, November 4, 1978
6. *Los Angeles Times*, November 4, 1978
7. *Los Angeles Times*, November 4, 1978
8. *Los Angeles Times*, November 4, 1978
9. *Los Angeles Times*, November 4, 1978
10. *Los Angeles Times*, November 4, 1978
11. *Los Angeles Times*, November 4, 1978
12. *Los Angeles Times*, November 4, 1978
13. *Los Angeles Times*, November 4, 1978
14. *Fresno Bee*, November 5, 1978
15. *Fresno Bee*, April 14, 1979
16. *Fresno Bee*, April 14, 1979
17. *Fresno Bee*, July 11, 1981
18. *Fresno Bee*, July 11, 1981
19. *Fresno Bee*, July 11, 1981
20. *Fresno Bee*, July 11, 1981
21. *Fresno Bee*, July 7, 1981
22. *Fresno Bee*, July 11, 1981
23. *Fresno Bee*, July 11, 1981
24. *Fresno Bee*, July 15, 1981 V
25. *Fresno Bee*, August 23, 1981
26. *Fresno Bee*, January 21, 1982

Chapter Seven — A Few Judicious Remarks

1. Inquiry Concerning a Judge No. 43, Report of the Special Panel to the Commission on Judicial Performance, August 7, 1980
2. Inquiry Concerning a Judge No. 43
3. Inquiry Concerning a Judge No. 43
4. *Sacramento Union*, July 15, 1977
5. Inquiry Concerning a Judge No. 43
6. *Los Angeles Herald Examiner*, October 22, 1979
7. *Los Angeles Herald Examiner*, October 22, 1979
8. *Los Angeles Herald Examiner*, October 22, 1979
9. Inquiry Concerning a Judge No. 43
10. Inquiry Concerning a Judge N0. 43
11. *Fresno Bee*, October 17, 1979
12. Inquiry Concerning a Judge No. 43
13. *Los Angeles Herald Examiner*, October 22, 1979
14. *Los Angeles Herald Examiner*, October 22, 1979
15. *Los Angeles Herald Examiner*, October 22, 1979
16. *Los Angeles Herald Examiner*, October 17, 1979
17. *Los Angeles Herald Examiner*, October 22, 1979
18. *Los Angeles Herald Examiner*, October 22, 1979
19. *Los Angeles Herald Examiner*, October 22, 1979
20. *Los Angeles Herald Examiner*, October 22, 1979

21. *Los Angeles Herald Examiner*, October 22, 1979
22. *Los Angeles Herald Examiner*, October 22, 1979
23. *Los Angeles Herald Examiner*, October 22, 1979
24. *Los Angeles Herald Examiner*, October 22, 1979
25. Inquiry Concerning a Judge No. 43

Chapter Eight — Judicial Indiscretion

1. *Los Angeles Times*, August 6, 1981
2. *Los Angeles Times*, August 6, 1981
3. *Los Angeles Times*, August 5, 1981
4. *Los Angeles Times*, August 13, 1981
5. *Los Angeles Times*, August 18, 1981
6. *San Diego Union*, September 26, 1981
7. *Los Angeles Times*, August 5, 1981
8. *San Diego Union*, October 9, 1981
9. *Los Angeles Times*, October 15, 1981
10. *San Diego Union*, October 15, 1981
11. *Santa Ana Register*, June 24, 1982
12. *Santa Ana Register*, August 5, 1982
13. *Santa Ana Register*, August 5, 1982

Chapter Nine — Two Whites Don't Make It Right

1. *Oakland Tribune*, February 6, 1982
2. *Oakland Tribune*, February 6, 1982, letter from Robert E. Foster, President of the Oakland Police Officers' Association
3. See Foster letter, note 2
4. *Oakland Tribune*, February 6, 1982
5. *Oakland Tribune*, February 5, 1982
6. *Oakland Tribune*, February 5, 1982
7. *Oakland Tribune*, February 5, 1982
8. *Oakland Tribune*, February 5, 1982
9. *Oakland Tribune*, February 5, 1982
10. *Oakland Tribune*, February 5, 1982
11. *Oakland Tribune*, February 5, 1982
12. *Oakland Tribune*, February 6, 1982
13. *Oakland Tribune*, February 6, 1982
14. *Oakland Tribune*, February 1, 1982
15. *Oakland Tribune*, February 1, 1982
16. *Oakland Tribune*, February 1, 1982
17. *Oakland Tribune*, February 1, 1982
18. *Oakland Tribune*, February 1, 1982

Chapter Ten — "The Judge Criminals Love"

1. *Oakland Tribune*, May 2, 1982
2. *Oakland Tribune*, May 2, 1982
3. *Courts and Judges*, Sage Publications
4. Richmond (California) Police Department, Offense Report, Dated: August 22, 1968
5. Richmond Police Department, Offense Report, Supplemental or Continuation Report, Dated: September 24, 1968
6. Richmond Police Department, Offense Report, Dated: November 26, 1968
7. Richmond Police Department, Offense Report, Dated: November 26, 1968
8. *Oakland Tribune*, May 2, 1982

9. *Oakland Tribune*, May 2, 1982
10. *Oakland Tribune*, AP Wire story, May 5, 1982
11. *Oakland Tribune*, May 2, 1982
12. *Oakland Tribune*, May 2, 1982
13. *Oakland Tribune*, May 2, 1982
14. *Oakland Tribune*, May 2, 1982
15. *Oakland Tribune*, May 2, 1982 and *Los Angeles Times*, April 23, 1982

Chapter Eleven — Your Parents Are So Proud of You

1. *San Fernando Valley Daily News*, July 3, 1981
2. *Daily News*, July 3, 1981
3. *Daily News*, July 3, 1981
4. *Daily News*, July 3, 1981
5. *Daily News*, July 3, 1981
6. *Daily News*, July 3, 1981
7. *Daily News*, July 3, 1981
8. *Daily News*, February 11, 1982
9. 1974 political campaign reports filed by the Personal Freedom Political Fund filed with the California Secretary of State
10. *Daily News*, July 3, 1981
11. *Daily News*, July 3, 1981
12. *Daily News*, July 3, 1981
13. *Daily News*, July 3, 1981
14. *Daily News*, July 3, 1981
15. *Daily News*, July 3, 1981
16. *Daily News*, February 11, 1982
17. *Daily News*, July 3, 1981
18. *Daily News*, July 3, 1981
19. Telephone communications between the author and the office of the California State Bar

Chapter Twelve — Democracy In Action

1. *Sacramento Bee*, September 20, 1979
2. *San Francisco Chronicle*, March 9, 1982
   Los Angeles Herald Examiner, June 14, 1981
3. *San Francisco Chronicle*, March 9, 1982
4. *Sacramento Bee*, September 9, 1979
5. *San Francisco Chronicle*, March 9, 1982
6. *San Francisco Chronicle*, March 9, 1982
7. *Los Angeles Herald Examiner*, June 14, 1981
8. *Los Angeles Herald Examiner*, June 14, 1981
9. *Courts and Judges*, Sage Publications

Chapter Thirteen — Judges, Politics, and Money?

1. California Fair Political Practices Commission (FPPC) Report on the 1978 general election
2. See FPPC report, note 1
3. *Los Angeles Times*, August 28, 1979
4. Fact Force Press Release, 1978
5. FPPC reports on the 1978 primary and general elections
6. Letter from Mr. Frankel, Dated: September 4, 1981

Chapter Fourteen — Where Do They All Come From?

1. *Sacramento Bee*, October 7, 1979
2. *San Francisco Chronicle*, Herb Caen, October 5,   1979
3. *Escondido Daily Times Advocate*, August 10, 1978
4. *San Francisco Chronicle*, Herb Caen, October 5,   1979
5. *Sacramento Bee*, October 7, 1979
6. *Sacramento Bee*, October 7, 1979
7. *Los Angeles Times*, May 7, 1978
8. *New West*, "A Woman Scorned", January 1982
9. *Los Angeles Herald Examiner*; October 8, 1979
10. *Human Events*, September 19, 1981
11. *San Francisco Chronicle*, October 8, 1979
12. *New West*, January 1982
13. *New West*, January 1982
14. Stated by Rose Bird in a conversation with Stan Boyles, Idaho Attorney General's Office
15. *Oakland Tribune*, February 9, 1982
16. Capital News Service, March 17, 1980
17. *San Francisco Chronicle*, February 26, 1980
18. *San Francisco Sunday Examiner and Chronicle*, July 8, 1979
19. *San Francisco Sunday Examiner and Chronicle*, July 8, 1979
20. Civil case records of the Clerk of the Sacramento Superior Court
21. *Sacramento Union*, October 30, 1979
22. *Sacramento Union*, October 30, 1979
23. *San Francisco Sunday Examiner and Chronicle*, July 8, 1979
24. *Sacramento Bee*, April 6, 1977
25. *Los Angeles Herald Examiner*, October 8, 1979
26. *Los Angeles Times*, October 9, 1979
27. *Sacramento Bee*, September 25, 1982
28. *Oakland Tribune*, October 14, 1979

Chapter Fifteen — Bird Reigns Supreme

1. *New West*, January, 1982
2. *Judging Judges*, Preble Stoltz, The Free Press
3. *Judging Judges*
4. *Judging Judges*
5. Records of the Commission on Judicial Performance, re: The Tanner Decision
6. *Judging Judges*
7. Records of the Commission on Judicial Performance (see note 5)
8. Records of the Commission on Judicial Appointments, Hearings on the Appointment of Rose Bird as Chief Justice
9. *Judging Judges*
10. *Judging Judges*
11. *Judging Judges*
12. *Los Angeles Times*, July 7, 1979

Chapter Sixteen — Bird Consolidates Her Power

1. *Judging Judges*, Preble Stoltz, The Free Press
2. *Judging Judges*
3. Commission on Judicial Appointments Hearings on the Appointment of Rose Bird as Chief Justice

Chapter Seventeen — Cracking the Whip, Selectively

1. *Los Angeles Herald Examiner*, October 21, 1979
2. *Los Angeles Herald Examiner*, October 21, 1979
3. *Los Angeles Herald Examiner*, October 21, 1979
4. Records of the Commission on Judicial Performance, Special Investigation of the Supreme Court, re: The Tanner decision.

ChapterEighteen — We Take Care of Our Own

1. *Sacramento Union*, February 9, 1982
2. *Sacramento Union*, February 10, 1982
3. *Sacramento Union*, February 9, 1982
4. *Sacramento Union*, February 9, 1982
5. *Sacramento Union*, February 9, 1982
6. *Sacramento Union*, February 9, 1982
7. *Sacramento Union*, February 9, 1982
8. *Sacramento Union*, February 9, 1982
9. *Sacramento Union*, February 9, 1982
10. *Sacramento Union*, February 9, 1982
11. *Sacramento Union*, February 9, 1982
12. Dissent of Justices Clark and Richardson, the Caudillo decision.

Chapter Twenty Three — Judicial Tyranny

"Judicial Tyranny" by Clyde Small is an edited version of an article previously published in the Prosecutors Brief, a publication of the California District Attorneys' Association.

Chapter Twenty Four — How Court Decisions and Practices Hamper Prosecution

"How Court Decisions and Practices Hamper Prosecution" by Edwin Meese III, and William James is a re-written version of an article previously published in the *Los Angeles Daily Journal* and was included in the first edition (1982) by permission of the authors.